P9-EEB-410

Recipes: Russian Cooking

Contents

Foods of the World

TIME-LIFE BOOKS, NEW YORK

© 1969 Time Inc. All rights reserved. Published simultaneously in Canada.

FIRST COURSES

Baklazhannaia Ikra (*Caucasus*)
POOR MAN'S CAVIAR

To make about 3 cups

1 large eggplant (about 2 pounds)
1 cup finely chopped onions
6 tablespoons olive oil
½ cup finely chopped green pepper
1 teaspoon finely chopped garlic
2 large ripe tomatoes, peeled, seeded and finely chopped (*see borshch*

ukraïnsky, page 21)
½ teaspoon sugar
2 teaspoons salt
Freshly ground black pepper
2 to 3 tablespoons lemon juice
Dark rye or pumpernickel bread or sesame-seed crackers

Preheat the oven to 425°. Bake the eggplant on a rack in the center of the oven for about an hour, turning it over once or twice until it is soft and its skin is charred and blistered.

Meanwhile, cook the onions in 4 tablespoons of the oil over moderate heat for 6 to 8 minutes until they are soft but not brown. Stir in the green pepper and garlic and cook, stirring occasionally, for 5 minutes longer. With a rubber spatula scrape the contents of the skillet into a mixing bowl.

Remove the skin from the baked eggplant with a small, sharp knife, then chop the eggplant pulp finely, almost to a purée. Add it to the mixing bowl and stir in the tomatoes, sugar, salt and a few gridings of black pepper. Mix together thoroughly. Heat the remaining 2 tablespoons of oil in the skillet over moderate heat and pour in the eggplant mixture. Bring to a boil, stirring constantly, then turn the heat to low, cover the skillet and simmer for an hour. Remove the cover and cook an additional half hour, stirring from time to time, until all the moisture in the pan has evaporated and the mixture is thick enough to hold its shape in a spoon. Stir in 2 tablespoons of lemon juice and taste for seasoning, adding more salt, pepper and lemon juice to taste. Transfer the "caviar" to a mixing bowl and chill, covered with plastic wrap, until ready to serve. Serve on squares of bread or on sesame-seed crackers.

Beliashi *(Central Asia)*

KAZAKH FRIED PASTIES FILLED WITH MEAT

To serve 4

DOUGH

1 package active dry yeast

¼ teaspoon sugar

3 cups all-purpose flour

1 cup lukewarm milk (110° to 115°)

Sprinkle the yeast and sugar over ¼ cup of the lukewarm milk in a small bowl. Let the mixture stand for 2 or 3 minutes, then stir to dissolve the yeast completely. Set the bowl in a warm, draft-free place (such as an unlighted oven) for 5 to 8 minutes, or until the mixture doubles in volume.

Pour the flour into a deep mixing bowl, and make a well in the center. Pour in the yeast mixture and the remaining milk and gradually stir the flour into the liquid. Then beat vigorously until a firm dough is formed. Gather the dough into a ball and place it on a lightly floured surface. Knead it by pressing down and pushing it forward several times with the heel of your hand, then fold it back on itself. Repeat for about 10 minutes, or until it is smooth and elastic. Shape the dough into a ball and place it in a large lightly buttered bowl. Dust the top with flour, cover loosely with a kitchen towel and set aside in the warm, draft-free place for about 45 minutes, or until the dough doubles in bulk.

FILLING

1½ pounds beef, finely ground

¾ cup finely chopped onions

1 teaspoon salt

¼ teaspoon freshly ground black pepper

3 to 4 tablespoons butter

2 to 3 tablespoons vegetable oil

Combine the meat, onions, salt and pepper in a large bowl and knead with your hands or beat with a large spoon until smooth. On a lightly floured surface roll the dough into a circle about ⅛ inch thick, then cut out 16 circles with a 4½-inch cookie cutter. Place 5 teaspoons of filling on each circle and moisten the edges of the dough with cold water. Fold up all the edges of the dough, enclosing the filling and making a flat, round cake.

Preheat the oven to 250°. In a 10- to 12-inch heavy skillet set over high heat, melt 3 tablespoons of butter in 2 tablespoons of oil. When the fat begins to turn light brown, add half of the flat cakes and cover the pan. Reduce the heat to moderate and cook for about 10 minutes on each side, or until the cakes are crisp and brown. Then transfer them to an ovenproof platter and keep warm in the low oven while you cook the remaining cakes. Add additional butter and oil to the pan if necessary. Serve at once.

Baklazhan Farshirovanny *(Russia)*
BAKED STUFFED EGGPLANT HALVES

To serve 2 to 4

2 tablespoons plus ½ cup vegetable
   oil
¼ cup finely chopped onions
1 teaspoon finely chopped garlic
2 medium tomatoes, peeled, seeded
   and coarsely chopped *(see borshch*
   ukrainsky, page 21)
4½ teaspoons salt
Freshly ground black pepper
Pinch of sugar

A 1½-pound firm eggplant
2 tablespoons finely shredded white
   cabbage
2 tablespoons scraped, finely diced
   carrots
¼ cup fresh white bread crumbs,
   made from homemade-style white
   bread, pulverized in a blender or
   finely shredded with a fork
2 tablespoons butter, cut into bits

Heat the 2 tablespoons of vegetable oil in a 10- to 12-inch heavy skillet over high heat until a light haze forms above it. Add 1 tablespoon of the onions and the teaspoon of garlic and reduce the heat to moderate. Stirring frequently, cook for 3 to 4 minutes, or until the onions are soft and golden brown. Stir in the tomatoes, ½ teaspoon of the salt, a few grindings of pepper and sugar, cover the pan and raise the heat to high. Cook for 2 or 3 minutes, then cook briskly, uncovered, until all the liquid has evaporated and the sauce is thick enough to barely hold its shape in a spoon.

Cut the eggplant in half lengthwise and with a small, sharp knife, make a long, ½-inch-deep incision into the flesh. Be careful not to pierce the skin. Sprinkle the cut sides of the eggplant halves evenly with 3 teaspoons of the salt and let them rest for ½ hour. Then wash the halves under cold water to remove the salt, and pat them thoroughly dry with paper towels.

In a heavy, 10- to 12-inch skillet, heat the remaining ½ cup of oil over high heat until a light haze forms above it. Place the eggplant halves in the pan flesh-side down, and reduce the heat to moderate. Fry 10 minutes, then turn the eggplant over with a spatula, cover the pan and cook 10 minutes longer. Drain the eggplant flesh-side down on paper towels.

Add the remaining onions and the carrots and cabbage to the oil still in the pan. Cook uncovered over moderate heat for 3 to 5 minutes, or until the vegetables are tender but not brown.

Carefully scoop the flesh out of the eggplant halves, leaving a ½-inch layer of the flesh intact in the shells. Chop the pulp finely, add it to the vegetables in the skillet and stir in 1 tablespoon of the tomato sauce and the remaining 1 teaspoon of salt. Stirring constantly, cook uncovered over moderate heat for 5 minutes, or until the mixture is thoroughly heated.

Preheat the oven to 350°. Spoon the filling into the eggplant halves, dividing it evenly between them. Arrange the stuffed shells side by side in a shallow baking dish just large enough to hold them snugly in one layer. Spoon the remaining tomato sauce evenly over the top, sprinkle with the bread crumbs and dot with the bits of butter. Bake in the center of the oven for about 15 minutes, or until the filling is golden brown.

Serve as a luncheon dish or cut each half into halves again and serve as a first course or vegetable course.

Gutap *(Central Asia)*
DEEP-FRIED HERB FRITTERS

To serve 8 to 10

FILLING

10 tablespoons finely chopped scallions, including 2 inches of their green tops	Freshly ground black pepper
	8 tablespoons (¼-pound stick) butter
3 tablespoons finely chopped parsley	DOUGH
3 tablespoons finely cut fresh dill leaves	One half recipe for *samsa* dough *(page 88)*
1 teaspoon salt	Vegetable oil for deep-fat frying

In a mixing bowl, combine the chopped scallions, parsley and dill and toss them together with the salt and pepper. Cut the butter into tiny bits and chill until the dough is ready.

Prepare and cut the dough into 48 squares, following the directions for *samsa (page 88)*. Top each square of dough with 1 teaspoon of herb filling and a bit of the butter. Draw up the corners of the squares and pinch the corners firmly together, enclosing the filling.

Pour enough oil into a deep-frying saucepan or heavy, flameproof casserole to come 4 inches up the sides of the pan, and heat until it registers 375° on a deep-frying thermometer. Drop in the fritters, 10 or 12 at a time, and fry 3 or 4 minutes, or until they are crisp and golden. Remove them from the oil with a slotted spoon and drain them on paper towels while you fry and drain the remaining fritters similarly. Serve at once, as an accompaniment to cocktails or tea.

Bliny *(Russia)*
BUCKWHEAT PANCAKES

"Bliny" have a distinctive taste quite unlike the average griddlecake, mainly because they are made with a yeast batter. Their preparation should start about 6 hours before you plan to serve them. When the batter is complete, the pancakes must be cooked and served at once.

To serve 6 to 8

½ cup lukewarm water (110° to 115°)
1½ packages active dry yeast
½ cup buckwheat flour
2 cups white all-purpose flour
2 cups lukewarm milk (110° to 115°)
3 egg yolks, lightly beaten
½ teaspoon salt

1 teaspoon sugar
½ pound butter, melted and cooled
2 cups sour cream (1 pint)
3 egg whites

16 ounces red or black caviar or substitute 1 pound thinly sliced smoked salmon, sturgeon or herring fillets

Pour the lukewarm water into a small, shallow bowl and sprinkle the yeast over it. Let the yeast stand 2 or 3 minutes, then stir to dissolve it completely. Set in a warm, draft-free spot (such as an unlighted oven) for 3 to 5 minutes, or until the mixture almost doubles in volume.

In a large mixing bowl, combine ¼ cup of the buckwheat flour and the 2 cups of white flour. Make a deep well in the center and pour in 1 cup of the lukewarm milk and the yeast mixture. Slowly stir the flour into the liquid ingredients with a large wooden spoon, then beat vigorously until the mixture is smooth. Cover the bowl loosely with a towel and set it aside in the warm, draft-free spot for 3 hours, or until the mixture doubles in volume.

Stir the batter thoroughly and vigorously beat in the remaining ¼ cup of buckwheat flour. Cover with a towel and let the batter rest in the warm draft-free spot another 2 hours. Again stir the batter and gradually beat in the remaining cup of lukewarm milk and the 3 egg yolks, salt, sugar, 3 tablespoons of the melted butter and 3 tablespoons of the sour cream.

With a whisk or a rotary or electric beater, beat the egg whites in a large bowl until they form stiff, unwavering peaks on the beater when it is lifted from the bowl. With a rubber spatula, fold the egg whites gently but thoroughly into the batter, cover loosely with a towel, and let the batter rest in the warm, draft-free spot for 30 minutes.

Preheat the oven to 200°. With a pastry brush, lightly coat the bottom of a 10- to 12-inch skillet (preferably with a nonstick surface) with melted butter. Set the pan over high heat until a drop of water flicked across its surface evaporates instantly. Pour in about 3 tablespoons of the batter for each pan-

6

cake (you will be able to make about 3 at a time, each about 3 or 4 inches wide) and fry 2 or 3 minutes, then brush the top lightly with butter. With a spatula or your fingers, turn the pancake over and cook another 2 minutes, or until golden brown. Transfer the pancakes to an ovenproof dish and keep them warm in the oven while you fry the remaining pancakes similarly, adding additional butter to the pan as needed.

Serve the *bliny* hot, accompanied by bowls of the remaining butter and the sour cream. Traditionally, the *bliny* are spread with melted butter and a mound of red caviar or slice of smoked fish, then topped with a spoonful of sour cream. If you are serving black caviar, omit the sour cream.

Pochki v Madere (*Russia*)
KIDNEYS IN MADEIRA SAUCE

To serve 4

4 veal kidneys, trimmed of their knobs of fat	1 cup Madeira wine
	6 tablespoons sour cream
¼ cup all-purpose flour	2 teaspoons salt
4 tablespoons butter	¼ teaspoon freshly ground black pepper

Cut the kidneys crosswise into ½-inch-thick slices. Dip the slices in flour one at a time and shake them vigorously to rid them of any excess flour. Melt the butter in a 10- to 12-inch enameled or stainless-steel skillet over high heat. When the butter begins to brown, drop in the kidneys and, stirring them frequently, cook 2 or 3 minutes on each side, or until they are lightly browned.

With a slotted spoon or tongs, transfer the kidneys to a heated plate and pour the Madeira into the pan. Raise the heat to high and boil briskly, meanwhile scraping in any brown particles clinging to the bottom of the pan. Continue to boil briskly, uncovered, until the wine has cooked down to about ½ cup. Reduce the heat to low and, with a whisk, beat in the sour cream, a tablespoon at a time. Return the kidneys to the pan, stir to coat them thoroughly with the sauce, and simmer another minute or so to heat them through. Sprinkle with salt and pepper, taste for seasoning, and serve at once, as a first course or on a *zakuska* table.

Vatrushki *(Russia)*
POT-CHEESE TARTLETS

To serve 6 to 8

DOUGH

1¾ cups all-purpose flour	1 egg
½ teaspoon baking powder	½ cup sour cream
½ teaspoon salt	4 tablespoons unsalted butter

DOUGH: Sift the flour, baking powder and salt into a large mixing bowl. Make a deep well in the center of the flour and drop in the egg, sour cream and butter. With your fingers, slowly mix the flour into the liquid ingredients, then beat vigorously with a wooden spoon until a smooth, moderately firm dough is formed. Gather the dough into a ball, wrap it loosely in wax paper, and chill for at least 30 minutes.

FILLING

1 pound large-curd pot cheese	½ teaspoon sugar
1 tablespoon sour cream	½ teaspoon salt
2 eggs	1 egg yolk mixed with 1 tablespoon cold water

FILLING: Drain the cheese by placing it in a colander, covering it with a double thickness of cheesecloth or a kitchen towel and weighting it with a heavy dish. Let it drain undisturbed for 2 or 3 hours, then with the back of a large spoon, rub the cheese through a fine sieve set over a large bowl. Beat into it the sour cream, eggs, sugar and salt. Chill for at least 30 minutes.

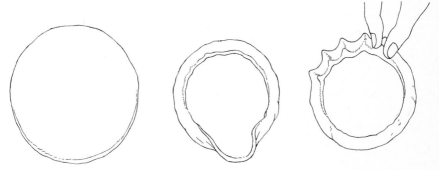

Preheat the oven to 400°. On a lightly floured surface, roll the dough into a circle about ⅛ inch thick. With a 4-inch cookie cutter, cut out as many circles as possible. Gather the remaining scraps into a ball, roll it out again, and cut out additional circles (there should be 14 to 16 circles in all). Make a border around each circle by turning over about ¼ inch of the dough all around its circumference and pinching this raised rim into small decorative pleats *(see drawings opposite)*. Drop 1½ tablespoons of filling into the center and flatten it slightly. Using a pastry brush, coat the filling and borders with the egg yolk-and-water mixture and bake in the center of the oven for 20 minutes, or until a pale gold. Serve the *vatrushki* as an accompaniment to soup, or alone as a first course.

Pashtet *(Russia)*
LIVER PÂTÉ

To serve 6 to 8

¼ cup vegetable oil
1 pound calf's or baby beef liver, carefully trimmed and cut into ½-inch dice
2 tablespoons unsalted butter
1 carrot, scraped and coarsely chopped
1 cup coarsely chopped onions

1 tablespoon finely chopped parsley
1½ teaspoons salt
⅛ teaspoon finely ground black pepper
⅛ teaspoon ground nutmeg
8 tablespoons unsalted butter, softened (¼-pound stick)
4 hard-cooked eggs, peeled and halved

In a heavy 10- to 12-inch skillet, heat the oil over high heat until a light haze forms above it. Drop in the calf or beef liver and, stirring constantly, fry until the pieces are golden brown. With a rubber spatula scrape the liver into a mixing bowl.

Melt the 2 tablespoons of butter in the same skillet and add the carrot and onions. Cook uncovered over moderate heat, stirring occasionally, until the vegetables are soft but not brown, then add them to the liver in the bowl. Stir in the chopped parsley and put the entire mixture through the finest blade of a meat grinder.

With a large spoon, beat in the salt, pepper and nutmeg, then beat in the 8 tablespoons of butter, 1 tablespoon at a time. Purée the mixture through the finest blade of a food mill and taste for seasoning. Spoon the pâté into a 1- to 1½-quart mold, smooth the top and cover with plastic wrap. Refrigerate for at least 8 hours, or until firm.

Serve the pâté directly from the mold or, if you prefer, unmold the pâté in the following fashion: Run a knife around the edge of the mold and invert a flat plate on top. Grasp the plate and mold firmly together and turn them over. The pâté should slide out easily. Surround the pâté with the hard-cooked egg halves and serve as a first course, in an open sandwich, or on the *zakuska* table.

Constructing the Classic "Kulebiaka"

A delicate filling of salmon, mushrooms, onions, rice, eggs and herbs is mounded high on a 7-by-16-inch rectangle of dough that has been set on a buttered cookie sheet. With a pastry brush, coat the exposed rim of dough with an egg yolk-and-cream mixture, then drape a 9-by-18-inch rectangle of dough over a rolling pin *(below)* and unroll it over the filling.

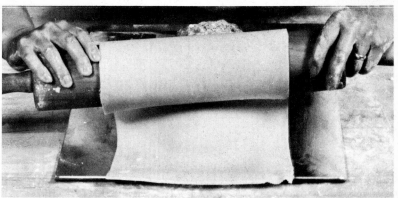

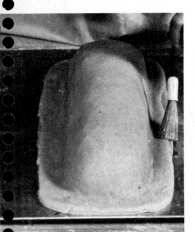

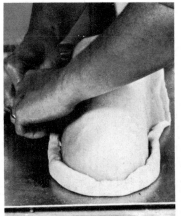

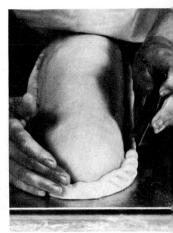

One way of sealing the loaf is to brush the edges gently with the yolk-and-cream mixture.

Turn up the border of dough to make a shallow rim around filling. Try not to stretch the dough.

With a pastry crimper, pinch the rim in narrow pleats (or simply make shallow cuts with a knife).

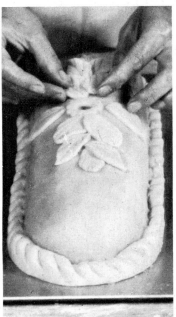

If you like, you may gather any remaining pastry scraps into a ball, roll them out again and, with a cookie cutter, cut out such decorative shapes as leaves *(far left)*. Use a small knife to make leaf veinings on the dough. Cut out a small circle from the center of the loaf and brush the entire surface of the loaf with the egg yolk-and-cream mixture. Then arrange the pastry leaves around the opening *(left)* and refrigerate before baking.

Kulebiaka (Russia)

FLAKY SALMON OR CABBAGE LOAF

To serve 8 to 10

PASTRY
4 cups all-purpose flour
½ pound chilled unsalted butter,
   cut into bits

6 tablespoons chilled vegetable
   shortening
1 teaspoon salt
10 to 12 tablespoons ice water

PASTRY: In a large, chilled bowl, combine the flour, butter, shortening and salt. Working quickly, use your fingertips to rub the flour and fat together until they blend and resemble flakes of coarse meal. Pour 10 tablespoons of the water over the mixture all at once, toss together lightly and gather into a ball. If the dough seems crumbly, add up to 2 tablespoons more ice water by drops. Divide the dough in half, dust each half with flour, and wrap them separately in wax paper. Refrigerate 3 hours, or until firm.

SALMON FILLING
2 cups dry white wine
1 cup coarsely chopped onions
½ cup coarsely chopped celery
1 cup scraped, coarsely chopped
   carrots
10 whole black peppercorns
4½ teaspoons salt
2½ pounds fresh salmon, in one
   piece
8 tablespoons unsalted butter (¼-
   pound stick)

½ pound fresh mushrooms, thinly
   sliced
3 tablespoons fresh, strained lemon
   juice
Freshly ground black pepper
3 cups finely chopped onions
½ cup unconverted, long-grain white
   rice
1 cup chicken stock, fresh or canned
⅓ cup finely cut fresh dill leaves
3 hard-cooked eggs, finely chopped

SALMON FILLING: Combine 3 quarts of water, the wine, the coarsely chopped onion, celery, carrots, peppercorns, and 3 teaspoons of the salt in a 4- to 6-quart enameled or stainless-steel casserole. Bring to a boil over high heat, then lower the salmon into the liquid and reduce the heat to low. Simmer 8 to 10 minutes, or until the fish is firm to the touch. With a slotted spatula, transfer the fish to a large bowl and separate it into small flakes with your fingers or a fork.

Melt 2 tablespoons of the butter in a heavy 10- to 12-inch skillet set over high heat. Add the mushrooms, reduce the heat to moderate, and, stirring occasionally, cook for 3 to 5 minutes, or until the mushrooms are soft. With a slotted spoon, transfer the mushrooms to a small bowl and toss them with lemon juice, ½ teaspoon of salt and a few grindings of pepper.

Melt 4 more tablespoons of butter in the skillet over high heat and drop in all but 1 tablespoon of the finely chopped onions. Reduce the heat to moderate and, stirring occasionally, cook 3 to 5 minutes, or until the onions are soft but not brown. Stir in the remaining 1 teaspoon of salt and ¼ teaspoon of pepper and with a rubber spatula, scrape into the mushrooms.

Now melt the remaining 2 tablespoons of butter in the skillet over high heat. Drop in the remaining tablespoon of chopped onion, reduce the heat to moderate and stirring frequently, cook for 2 to 3 minutes, or until soft but not brown. Stir in the rice and cook 2 or 3 minutes, stirring almost constantly, until each grain is coated with butter. Pour in the chicken stock, bring to a boil, and cover the pan tightly. Reduce the heat to low and simmer for 12 minutes, or until the water is completely absorbed and the rice is tender and fluffy. Off the heat, stir in the dill with a fork. Add the cooked mushrooms and onions, rice and chopped, hard-cooked eggs to the bowl of salmon and toss together lightly but thoroughly. Taste for seasoning.

CABBAGE FILLING
3-pound head of white cabbage, quartered, cored, then coarsely shredded
4 tablespoons butter
2 large onions, coarsely chopped

4 hard-cooked eggs, finely chopped
¼ cup finely cut fresh dill leaves
2 tablespoons finely chopped parsley
1 tablespoon salt
½ teaspoon sugar
Freshly ground black pepper

CABBAGE FILLING: Over high heat, bring 4 quarts of lightly salted water to a boil in an 8- to 10-quart pot and drop in the cabbage. Reduce the heat to moderate and cook uncovered for 5 minutes. Then drain the cabbage in a colander and set it aside.

Melt the butter over high heat in a deep skillet or 3- to 4-quart casserole. Add the chopped onions, reduce the heat to moderate, and cook 5 to 8 minutes, or until the onions are soft and lightly colored. Drop in the cabbage and cover the pan. (The pan may be filled to the brim, but the cabbage will shrink as it cooks.) Simmer over low heat for 30 to 40 minutes, or until the cabbage is tender, then uncover the pan, raise the heat to high and boil briskly until almost all of the liquid in the pan has evaporated. Drain the cabbage in a collander and combine it with the chopped eggs, dill and parsley. Stir in the salt, sugar and a few grindings of pepper and taste for seasoning.

2 tablespoons butter, softened
1 egg yolk, mixed with 1 tablespoon cream

1 tablespoon butter, melted
1 cup melted butter, hot but not brown, or sour cream

TO ASSEMBLE: Preheat the oven to 400°. Place one ball of dough on a floured surface and roll it into a rough rectangle about 1 inch thick. Dust with flour and roll until the dough is about ⅛ inch thick, then trim it to a rectangle 7 inches wide by 16 inches long.

Coat a large cookie sheet with 2 tablespoons of butter, drape the pastry over the rolling pin and unroll it over the cookie sheet. Place the filling along the length of the pastry, leaving a 1-inch border of dough exposed around it. With a pastry brush, brush the exposed rim of dough with the egg-yolk-and-cream mixture. Roll the other half of the dough into a rectangle about 9 inches wide and 18 inches long, drape over the pin and unroll over the filling. Seal the edges by pressing down hard with the back of a fork. Or use your fingertips or a pastry crimper to pinch the edges into narrow pleats. Cut out a 1-inch circle from the center of the dough. If you like you may gather any remaining pastry scraps into a ball, roll them out again, and with a cookie cutter or small, sharp knife, cut out decorative shapes such as leaves or triangles and decorate the top of the loaf. Coat the entire surface of the pastry with the remaining egg-yolk-and-cream mixture, place any pastry shapes on top, and refrigerate for 20 minutes. Pour 1 tablespoon of melted butter into the opening of the loaf and bake the *kulebiaka* in the center of the oven for 1 hour, or until golden brown. Serve at once, accompanied by a pitcher of melted butter or sour cream.

Pirozhki *(Russia)*
SMALL PASTRIES FILLED WITH MEAT

To make about 40

PASTRY
4 cups all-purpose flour
½ teaspoon salt
16 tablespoons (two ¼-pound sticks) unsalted butter, cut into ¼-inch bits and chilled
8 tablespoons chilled lard, cut into ¼-inch bits
8 to 12 tablespoons ice water

PASTRY: Combine the flour, salt, butter and lard in a deep bowl. With your fingers, rub the flour and fat together until they look like flakes of coarse meal. Pour in 8 tablespoons of ice water all at once and gather the dough into a ball. If it crumbles, add up to 4 tablespoons more ice water, a tablespoon at a time, until the particles adhere. Wrap the ball in wax paper, and chill for about 1 hour. On a lightly floured surface, shape the pastry into a rough rectangle 1 inch thick and roll it into a strip about 21 inches long and 6 inches wide. Fold the strip into thirds to make a 3-layered packet 7 inches long and 6 inches wide. Turn the pastry around and again roll it out lengthwise into a 21-by-6-inch strip. Fold into thirds and roll out the packet as before. Repeat this entire process twice more, ending with the folded packet. Wrap it in wax paper and refrigerate for at least 1 hour.

FILLING
4 tablespoons butter
3 cups finely chopped onions
1½ pounds lean ground beef
3 hard-cooked eggs, finely chopped

6 tablespoons finely cut fresh dill leaves
2 teaspoons salt
¼ teaspoon freshly ground black pepper

FILLING: Over high heat, melt the butter in a heavy 10- to 12-inch skillet. Add the onions and, stirring occasionally, cook over moderate heat for 8 to 10 minutes, or until they are soft and transparent but not brown. Stir in the beef and, mashing the meat with a fork to break up any lumps, cook briskly until no traces of pink remain. Grind the meat-and-onion mixture through the finest blade of a meat grinder (or, lacking a grinder, chop the mixture finely). Combine the meat in a large bowl with the eggs, dill, salt and pepper, mix thoroughly and taste for seasoning.

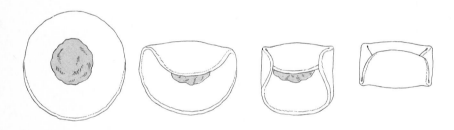

Preheat the oven to 400°. On a lightly floured surface, roll the dough into a circle about ⅛ inch thick. With a 3- to 3½-inch cookie cutter, cut out as many circles as you can. Gather the scraps into a ball and roll out again, cutting additional circles. Drop 2 tablespoons of filling in the center of each round and flatten the filling slightly. Fold one long side of the dough up over the filling, almost covering it. Fold in the two ends of the dough about ½ inch, and lastly, fold over the remaining long side of dough. Place the *pirozhki* side by side, with the seam sides down on a buttered baking sheet. Bake for 30 minutes, or until golden brown. Serve with clear chicken or beef soup, on the *zakuska* table or presented alone as a first course.

Yarpakh Dolmasy *(Caucasus)*

GRAPEVINE LEAVES STUFFED WITH LAMB AND RICE

To serve 4 to 6

3 tablespoons butter
1 cup finely chopped onions
¼ cup unconverted long-grain, white rice
½ pound ground lean lamb
1 tablespoon finely chopped fresh coriander *(cilantro)*
2 tablespoons finely cut fresh dill leaves
1 tablespoon finely cut fresh mint,
1 tablespoon powdered cinnamon

or substitute ½ teaspoon dried mint
¼ cup fresh peas or thoroughly defrosted frozen peas
½ teaspoon salt
Freshly ground black pepper
28 pickled grapevine leaves (about 4 ounces)
2 cups chicken stock, fresh or canned
1 pint unflavored yoghurt

Melt the butter in a 10- to 12-inch skillet set over moderate heat. Add the onions, lower the heat and cook, stirring frequently, for 3 to 5 minutes, or until they are soft and lightly colored. Transfer them to a large bowl.

Bring 2 cups of water to a boil in a 1½- to 2-quart saucepan set over high heat. Stir in the rice, lower the heat and cook uncovered for 8 minutes, then drain through a sieve. Stir the rice, lamb, coriander, dill, mint, peas, salt and a few grindings of pepper into the onions and toss all the ingredients together lightly but thoroughly. Taste for seasoning.

Bring 4 cups of water to a boil in a 1½- to 2-quart saucepan and drop in the vine leaves. Boil briskly for 3 or 4 minutes, uncovered, then drain and pat the leaves thoroughly dry with paper towels. One at a time, place the leaves rough-side up on a flat surface, stem-sides facing you. Heap 2 teaspoons of filling in the center of the leaf and bring up both rounded sides, so that they meet in the middle, thus enclosing the filling. Then beginning at the far side, roll the vine leaf into a loose cylinder, tucking in the ends as you do and allowing enough slack for the rice to expand as it cooks.

Arrange the rolls, seam-side down, in a shallow casserole just large enough to hold them in one layer. Pack them in snugly side by side so that they retain their shape while cooking. Pour in the chicken stock and bring to a boil over high heat. Cover the casserole tightly, lower the heat, and simmer undisturbed for about 45 minutes.

Serve the vine rolls with a bowl of yoghurt sprinkled with cinnamon.

SOUPS

Borshch Moskovskii (Russia)
MOSCOW-STYLE BEET SOUP

To serve 6 to 8

2 tablespoons butter
½ cup finely chopped onions
1½ pounds beets, peeled and cut
   into strips ⅛ inch wide by 2
   inches long (about 5 cups)
¼ cup red wine vinegar
1 teaspoon sugar
2 tomatoes, peeled, seeded and
   coarsely chopped *(see borshch
   ukraïnsky, page 21)*
2 teaspoons salt
Freshly ground black pepper
2 quarts beef stock *(see shchi, page 20)*

½ pound white cabbage, quartered,
   cored and coarsely shredded
¼ pound boiled ham, cut into 1-
   inch cubes
¼ pound all-beef frankfurters, cut
   into ½-inch-thick rounds
1 pound boiled brisket from the
   stock, cut into 1-inch cubes
4 sprigs parsley, tied together with
   1 bay leaf
½ cup finely cut fresh dill or
   chopped parsley
1 cup sour cream

In a 6- to 8-quart pot, melt the butter over moderate heat. Add the onions and, stirring frequently, cook 3 to 5 minutes, or until they are soft but not brown. Stir in the beets, then add the wine vinegar, sugar, chopped tomatoes, 1 teaspoon of the salt and a few grindings of black pepper. Pour in ½ cup of the stock, cover the pan and simmer undisturbed for 50 minutes.

Pour the remaining stock into the pot and add the chopped cabbage. Bring to a boil, then stir in the ham, frankfurters and beef. Submerge the tied parsley and bay leaf in the soup, add another teaspoon of salt, and simmer, partially covered, for ½ hour.

Transfer the *borshch* to a large tureen and sprinkle with fresh dill or parsley. Accompany the soup with a bowl of sour cream, to be added to the *borshch* at the discretion of each diner.

Okroshka *(Russia)*

CHILLED VEGETABLE SOUP WITH MEAT

To serve 6 to 8

4 hard-cooked eggs
1 cup sour cream
2 teaspoons Dijon or Düsseldorf
    mustard
1 tablespoon salt
1 teaspoon sugar
6 cups *kvas (opposite)*, or less
    traditionally, substitute flat beer

¼ cup thinly sliced scallions,
    including 3 inches of their tops
1 medium cucumber, peeled, halved,
    seeded and cut into ¼-inch dice
½ pound boiled beef, cut into ¼-inch
    dice *(see shchi, page 20)*, or substitute
    ½ cup diced boiled ham or veal
3 tablespoons finely chopped parsley

With a large spoon, rub the eggs through a fine sieve set over a large bowl.
Beat in the sour cream, mustard, salt and sugar, then slowly beat in the *kvas*.
Add the scallions, cucumbers and meat, stir, and refrigerate before serving.
Taste for seasoning, sprinkle with parsley and serve in chilled soup bowls.

Botvinia *(Russia)*

GREEN VEGETABLE SOUP WITH FISH

To serve 6 to 8

1½ pounds fresh spinach leaves,
    stripped from the stems
1½ pounds fresh sorrel leaves,
    stripped from the stems
¼ cup scraped grated fresh
    horseradish root
6 tablespoons fresh strained lemon
    juice
1 tablespoon salt
¾ teaspoon sugar
6 cups *kvas (opposite)*

1½ cups finely sliced scallions,
    including ½ of the green stem
1 large cucumber, peeled, halved,
    seeded and cut into ¼-inch dice
    (1½ cups)
1½ pounds cold poached sturgeon
    or salmon *(see rybnaia solianka, page
    25)*, cut into 8 equal pieces
½ pound fresh crabmeat, or a
    7½-ounce can crabmeat, drained
    and free of all bits of shell and
    cartilage

Bring 3 quarts of water to a boil in a large pot and drop in the spinach and sorrel. Cook briskly, uncovered, for about 8 minutes, then drain the vegetables
in a colander or sieve and wash them quickly under cold running water. Purée the vegetables in a food mill or rub them with the back of a large spoon
through a fine sieve set over a large bowl. Cool to room temperature.

In a small bowl, combine the grated horseradish, lemon juice, salt and sugar. Stir into the vegetable purée and slowly stir in the *kvas*, ¼ cup at a time. Now stir in the scallions, cucumber, fish and crabmeat and taste for seasoning. Chill at least 2 hours before serving.

Kvas (*Russia*)
MINT-FLAVORED BREAD BEER

To make 6 cups

1 pound day-old black bread or
   Danish pumpernickel
2 tablespoons active dry yeast
1 cup sugar

¼ cup lukewarm water (110°-115°)
2 tablespoons fresh mint leaves or 1
   tablespoon crumbled dried mint
2 tablespoons raisins

Preheat the oven to 200°. Place the bread in the oven for about 1 hour, or until it is thoroughly dry. With a heavy knife, cut and chop it coarsely. Bring 6 quarts of water to a boil in an 8-quart casserole and drop in the bread. Remove from the heat, cover loosely with a kitchen towel, and set it aside for at least 8 hours. Strain the contents of the casserole through a fine sieve set over another large pot or bowl, pressing down hard on the soaked bread with the back of a large spoon before discarding it.

Sprinkle the yeast and ¼ teaspoon of the sugar over the ¼ cup of lukewarm water and stir to dissolve the yeast completely. Set aside in a warm, draft-free spot (such as an unlighted oven) for about 10 minutes, or until the mixture almost doubles in volume. Stir the yeast mixture, the remaining sugar and the mint into the strained bread water, cover with a towel, and set aside for at least 8 hours.

Strain the mixture again through a fine sieve set over a large bowl or casserole, then prepare to bottle it. You will need 2 to 3 quart-sized bottles, or a gallon jug. Pour the liquid through a funnel ⅔ of the way up the sides of the bottle. Then divide the raisins among the bottles and cover the top of each bottle with plastic wrap, secured with a rubber band. Place in a cool —but not cold—spot for 3 to 5 days, or until the raisins have risen to the top and the sediment has sunk to the bottom. Carefully pour off the clear amber liquid and rebottle it in the washed bottles. Refrigerate until ready to use. Although Russians drink *kvas* as a cold beverage, it may also be used as a cold-soup stock. (*See okroshka* and *botvinia, opposite.*)

Shchi *(Russia)*

CABBAGE SOUP

To serve 6 to 8

BEEF STOCK
1 pound fresh lean brisket of beef
5 pounds beef marrow bones, cracked
1 large onion, peeled and quartered

1 large carrot, scraped
2 celery tops, 6 sprigs of parsley
   and 2 bay leaves tied together
1 tablespoon salt

BEEF STOCK: In a heavy 6- to 8-quart pot, bring the pound of beef, beef bones and 4 quarts of water to a boil over high heat, skimming off any foam and scum as they rise to the surface. Add the onion, carrot, tied greens and salt, partially cover the pot and reduce the heat to low. Simmer 1 to 1½ hours, or until the meat is tender but not falling apart. Remove the meat from the pot with a slotted spoon, cut it into small dice and set the dice aside. Continue to simmer the stock partially covered, for about 4 hours longer. Then strain the stock through a fine sieve set over a large bowl, discarding the bones and greens. With a large spoon, skim off and discard as much of the surface fat as you can.

SOUP
4 tablespoons butter
2 cups thinly sliced onions
1½ pounds white cabbage, quartered,
   cored, then coarsely shredded
1 celery root, scraped and cut into
   fine strips
1 parsley root, scraped and cut into

fine strips
1 pound boiling potatoes, peeled
   and cut into ¼-inch dice (2½ cups)
4 medium tomatoes, peeled, seeded
   and chopped *(see borshch
   ukraïnsky, opposite)*
1 teaspoon salt
Freshly ground black pepper

SOUP: Melt the butter in a 3- to 4-quart pot set over high heat. Add the onions, reduce the heat to moderate, and cook 8 to 10 minutes, or until they are soft but not brown. Stir in the shredded cabbage and the celery and parsley roots, cover the pot, and simmer over low heat for 15 minutes.

Pour in the meat stock and add the reserved diced beef. Simmer over moderate heat (partially covered) for 20 minutes, then add the diced potatoes. Cook another 20 minutes and stir in the chopped tomatoes. Cook 10 minutes longer, then add the salt and a few grindings of pepper. Taste for seasoning. Serve hot, accompanied perhaps by *vatrushki (Recipe Index)*.

Borshch Ukraïnsky *(Ukraine)*
UKRAINE-STYLE BEET SOUP

To serve 6 to 8

4 medium tomatoes
4 tablespoons butter
1 cup finely chopped onions
2 cloves garlic, peeled and finely
  chopped
1 pound beets, trimmed of leaves
  and coarsely grated (2 cups)
½ celery root, peeled and coarsely
  grated (1 cup)
1 parsley root, peeled and coarsely
  grated (1 cup)
1 parsnip, peeled and coarsely grated
  (1 cup)

½ teaspoon sugar
¼ cup red wine vinegar
1 tablespoon salt
2 quarts beef stock, fresh *(see shchi,*
  opposite) or canned
1 pound boiling potatoes, peeled
  and cut into 1½-inch chunks
1 pound cabbage, cored and coarsely
  shredded
1 pound boiled brisket *(see shchi,*
  opposite), or 1 pound boiled ham,
  cut into 1-inch chunks
3 tablespoons finely chopped parsley
½ pint sour cream

Drop the tomatoes into boiling water for 15 seconds. Run them under cold water and peel them. Cut out the stem, then slice them in half crosswise. Squeeze the halves gently to remove the juices and seeds then chop them coarsely and set aside. In a heavy 10- to 12-inch skillet or casserole, melt the butter over moderate heat. Add the onions and garlic and, stirring frequently, cook 6 to 8 minutes, or until they are soft and lightly colored. Stir in the beets, celery root, parsley root, parsnip, half the tomatoes, the sugar, vinegar, salt and 1½ cups of the stock. Bring to a boil over high heat, then partially cover the pot and lower the heat. Simmer for 40 minutes.

Meanwhile, pour the remaining stock into a 6- to 8-quart casserole and add the potatoes and cabbage. Bring to a boil, then simmer partially covered for 20 minutes, or until the potatoes are tender but not falling apart. When the vegetable mixture has cooked its allotted time, add it to the casserole with the remaining tomatoes and the meat. Simmer partially covered for 10 to 15 minutes, until the *borshch* is heated. Taste for seasoning. Pour into a tureen, sprinkle with parsley and serve accompanied by sour cream.

Rassolnik *(Russia)*
TART SORREL SOUP WITH KIDNEYS

To serve 6

1 medium dill pickle
6 tablespoons butter
1 cup thinly sliced onions
½ cup finely chopped celery
1 cup finely chopped parsley
2 pounds fresh sorrel leaves, stripped
   from their stems, washed and
   coarsely chopped
¼ pound fresh spinach leaves,
   stripped from their stems, washed

and coarsely chopped
2 teaspoons salt
Freshly ground black pepper
2 quarts beef stock, fresh *(see shchi,*
   page 20) or canned
1 pound veal or lamb kidneys, well
   trimmed of their fat
½ cup flour
2 tablespoons vegetable oil
1 egg yolk
2 cups sour cream (optional)

Cut the pickle in half lengthwise and run a small spoon down its length to re-move the seeds and pulp. Place the seeds and pulp in a fine sieve set over a small bowl and press them firmly with the back of a spoon to extract all their juices before throwing them away. Set the juice aside, and chop the pick-le as finely as possible.

Melt 4 tablespoons of the butter in a 3- to 4-quart casserole over mod-erate heat. When the foam has almost subsided, stir in the onions and celery and cover the pan. Reduce the heat to low and simmer gently for at least 10 minutes, or until the onions are soft but not brown. Add the pickle, parsley, sorrel and spinach and stir in the salt and a few grindings of pepper. Pour in the beef stock, stir, and bring to a boil over high heat. Then reduce the heat to low, partially cover the pan, and simmer about 20 minutes.

While the soup is simmering, prepare the kidneys. With a small, sharp knife cut away their knobs of fat and slice the kidneys crosswise into pieces ½ inch thick. Dip the slices in the flour one at a time and shake them vig-orously to rid them of any excess flour. Heat the remaining 2 tablespoons of butter and the 2 tablespoons of oil in a heavy 10- to 12-inch skillet set over high heat. When the fat begins to turn light brown, add the kidneys. Stir-ring frequently, fry them briskly until they are lightly browned (the lamb kid-neys will take 2 or 3 minutes on each side, the veal kidneys 4 or 5 minutes). Do not overcook. With a slotted spoon, transfer the kidneys to the sim-mering soup. Pour off the fat in the skillet and in its place add 1 cup of the soup. Bring the soup to a boil, meanwhile scraping into it any browned bits clinging to the bottom of the pan. Pour the mixture into the soup and stir in the pickle juice.

In a mixing bowl, beat the egg yolk lightly with a fork. Slowly beat in 1 cup of the hot soup, then pour the egg mixture slowly into the casserole, stirring constantly. Simmer a moment or two without letting it come to a boil. Taste for seasoning, then serve the *rassolnik* directly from the casserole or in a large tureen.

You may either stir the sour cream into the soup directly before serving it or present it in a separate bowl to be added to each serving at the table.

Spas *(Caucasus)*
YOGHURT-AND-BARLEY SOUP WITH HERBS

To serve 6

¼ cup pearl barley	2 teaspoons salt
2 cups unflavored yoghurt (16 ounces)	2 teaspoons finely cut fresh mint leaves
4 eggs	2 teaspoons finely chopped fresh
2 tablespoons flour	coriander *(cilantro),* or substitute
2 tablespoons finely chopped onion	2 teaspoons finely chopped Italian
2 tablespoons butter	flat-leaf parsley

In a 1½- to 2-quart saucepan, bring 1 quart of water to a boil over high heat. Pour in the barley, reduce the heat and cook uncovered, stirring occasionally, for 45 minutes, or until the barley is tender but still intact. Drain the barley through a fine sieve and set it aside.

In a large mixing bowl, combine 1 quart cold water with the yoghurt and stir until dissolved. Break the eggs into a 3- to 4-quart saucepan and with a whisk, beat in the flour, a tablespoon at a time. Slowly whisk in the yoghurt mixture and place over high heat. Bring almost to a boil, whisking constantly, then lower the heat and simmer 2 to 3 minutes, or until the mixture thickens slightly. Do not let it boil. Stir in the barley, onions and butter, sprinkle with the salt, and simmer another minute. Pour into a heated tureen or individual bowls. Sprinkle with chopped mint and coriander (or parsley) and serve hot. To serve the soup cold, pour it into a large bowl, bring to room temperature, and chill at least 4 hours. Sprinkle with herbs just before serving.

Yaini *(Caucasus)*

BEEF SOUP WITH VEGETABLES AND APRICOTS

To serve 4 to 6

4 tablespoons butter
¼ cup finely chopped onions
2 medium tomatoes, peeled, seeded and coarsely chopped *(see borshch ukraïnsky, page 21)*
1 quart beef stock, fresh or canned
1 pound boiling potatoes, peeled and cut into 1-inch cubes (about 3 cups)

¼ cup dried apricots, cut into quarters
1½ teaspoons salt
⅛ teaspoon black pepper
1 pound boiled chuck or brisket of beef *(see shchi, page 20)* cut into 1-inch cubes
2 tablespoons finely chopped fresh coriander *(cilantro)*, or substitute Italian flat-leaf parsley

In a heavy 10- to 12-inch skillet, melt the butter over high heat. Add the onions and, stirring frequently, cook uncovered for 5 to 8 minutes, or until they are soft and lightly colored. Stir in the tomatoes and boil briskly, uncovered, until most of the liquid has evaporated and the mixture has thickened lightly. Stir in the beef stock. Then add the potatoes, apricots, salt and pepper, and bring to a boil over high heat. Reduce the heat to moderate, cover the pan and cook undisturbed for 20 minutes, or until the potatoes are tender but not falling apart. Stir in the cubed meat and simmer slowly for 10 minutes. Taste for seasoning. Transfer the stew to a large heated tureen or soup bowls, sprinkle with chopped coriander or parsley, and serve at once.

Chikhirtma *(Caucasus)*

TART CHICKEN SOUP WITH CORIANDER

To serve 8 to 10

A 4- to 4¼-pound stewing fowl
2 cups thinly sliced onions
½ teaspoon powdered saffron

4 eggs
½ cup fresh strained lemon juice
3 tablespoons coarsely chopped fresh coriander *(cilantro)*
Salt

In a heavy 6- to 8-quart pot, combine the stewing fowl, onions and enough cold water to cover the bird by 1 inch. Bring to a boil over high heat, meanwhile skimming off all the foam and scum with a large spoon as they rise to the surface. Stir in the saffron, cover the pan and reduce the heat to low. Simmer for about 2 hours, or until the bird is tender but not falling apart. Let the soup continue to simmer, and transfer the bird to a plate and with a small, sharp knife remove the skin. Cut the meat away from the bones and cut it into slivers. (You may add the meat to the finished soup or serve it separately. Alternatively refrigerate the meat, covered with plastic wrap, and use it in dishes such as *salat Olivier (Recipe Index.)*

In a small bowl beat the eggs just long enough to combine them. Then, beating with a wire whisk, slowly pour in 1 cup of the soup. Return the mixture to the simmering soup in a slow stream, whisking constantly. Simmer another minute or two or until the soup has thickened lightly. (Do not let it boil or it will curdle.) Stir in the lemon juice, taste for seasoning, and pour into a heated tureen. Sprinkle with coriander and serve at once.

Rybnaia Solianka (Russia)
FISH SOUP WITH ONIONS, CUCUMBERS AND TOMATOES

To serve 6 to 8

1 cup coarsely chopped onions	seeded and finely chopped
1 bay leaf	2 tomatoes, peeled, seeded and
2 sprigs parsley	coarsely chopped *(see borshch*
3 teaspoons salt	*ukraïnsky, page 21)*
2½ pounds sturgeon, halibut or	⅛ teaspoon white pepper
haddock steaks, cut 1 inch thick	4 teaspoons capers, drained and
4 tablespoons butter	washed under cold running water
2 cups thinly sliced onions	1 lemon, thinly sliced
1 medium cucumber, peeled, halved,	2 tablespoons finely chopped parsley
	12 black olives, pitted

In a 3- to 4-quart pot, combine 6½ cups of water, the onions, bay leaf, parsley and 1 teaspoon of the salt. Bring to a boil over high heat, then add the fish, lower the heat, and simmer gently, uncovered, for 6 minutes, until the fish is firm to the touch. Remove the fish and cut it into 1-inch chunks. Strain the fish stock through a fine sieve set over a bowl, pressing down on the onions and herbs with the back of a spoon before discarding them.

In a 2- to 3-quart casserole, melt the butter over high heat. Add the sliced onions, and cook 6 to 8 minutes until the onions are soft but not brown. Stir in the cucumbers and tomatoes and simmer 10 minutes. Pour in the strained fish stock, season with the remaining 2 teaspoons of salt and white pepper, and drop in the fish. Simmer gently a minute or two, until the soup and fish are heated through. Off the heat stir in the capers, lemon, parsley and olives. Taste for seasoning and serve directly from the casserole.

Ukha *(Russia)*

CLEAR FISH SOUP WITH LIME AND DILL

To serve 6

FISH STOCK	
2 cups sliced onions	⅛ teaspoon freshly ground black
1 bay leaf	pepper
6 whole black peppercorns	2½ to 3 pounds fish trimmings: the
3 sprigs parsley	spines, heads, or tails of any
1 teaspoon salt	white-fleshed fish
	2 egg whites

In a 3- to 4-quart enameled or stainless-steel casserole, combine 2 quarts of water with the onions, bay leaf, peppercorns, parsley, salt, pepper and fish trimmings. Bring to a boil over high heat, then reduce the heat to low and partially cover the casserole. Simmer undisturbed for 30 minutes.

Strain the stock through a fine sieve set over a large bowl. Press down hard on the vegetables and trimmings with the back of a large spoon to extract all their juices before discarding them. Return the stock to the casserole.

In a small bowl, beat the egg whites to a froth, add them to the stock, and bring the mixture to a boil over high heat, stirring constantly with a whisk. When the stock begins to froth and threatens to overflow the pan, remove it from the heat and let it rest about 5 minutes. Then slowly pour the entire contents of the pan into a cheesecloth-lined sieve set over a deep bowl. Let the stock drain through the sieve without disturbing it at any point. Discard the contents of the sieve and taste the stock for seasoning. It will doubtless need more salt.

FISH	
1 pound fish fillets: striped bass,	1 lime, thinly sliced
sea bass, or any other white-	1 tablespoon finely cut fresh dill
fleshed fish	leaves, or finely chopped parsley

Return the stock to the casserole and bring it to a boil over high heat. Drop in the fish fillets, reduce the heat to low, and simmer the fish uncovered for 3 to 4 minutes, or until it is firm to the touch and opaque. Do not overcook. With a slotted spoon, remove the fish from the casserole to a platter. Pour the soup into a heated tureen or individual soup bowls. Add the slices of the fish and lime, and sprinkle with the cut dill or chopped parsley. Serve at once.

Miasnaia Solianka *(Russia)*
MEAT SOUP WITH TOMATOES, ONIONS AND CUCUMBERS

To serve 6 to 8

6 cups beef stock, fresh or canned
¾ pound beef, preferably lean brisket, rump or bottom round, cut into ½-inch cubes
½ pound boneless shoulder of veal, trimmed of fat and cut into ½-inch cubes
4 tablespoons butter
2 cups thinly sliced onions
2 medium cucumbers, peeled, halved, seeded and cut into ¼-inch slices
2 large tomatoes, peeled, seeded and coarsely chopped *(see borshch ukraïnsky, page 21)*
1 teaspoon salt
Freshly ground black pepper
6 ounces boiled ham, sliced ½ inch thick
3 all-beef frankfurters, sliced into ½-inch rounds
12 black pitted olives
1 lemon, thinly sliced

In a heavy, 4- to 6-quart casserole, combine the beef stock, beef and veal. Bring to a boil over high heat, skimming the top of the foam and scum as they rise to the surface. Then partially cover the casserole, reduce the heat to moderate and simmer for about 1½ hours, or until the meat is tender enough to be easily pierced with a fork.

Meanwhile, melt 4 tablespoons of butter in a heavy, 10- to 12-inch skillet over high heat. Add the onions, reduce the heat to moderate and cook 3 to 5 minutes, or until the onions are soft but not brown. Drop in the cucumbers and cook, stirring occasionally, for about 10 minutes, or until they are tender but still slightly firm. Then stir in the chopped tomatoes and cook an additional 10 minutes. Season with the salt and a few grindings of black pepper, and transfer the contents of the skillet to the casserole. Add the ham and frankfurters and simmer 5 minutes, or until the meats are heated through.

Drop the olives into a saucepan of boiling water and boil briskly for 2 minutes. Drain and add them to the soup. Taste for seasoning, pour into a large heated tureen, and float the lemon slices on top. Serve at once.

SALADS VEGETABLES

Rossolye *(Baltic States)*

ESTONIAN VINAIGRETTE WITH HERRING AND BEETS

To serve 6 to 8

DRESSING

3 teaspoons powdered mustard

1¼ teaspoons sugar

1 to 2 tablespoons warm water

1 cup sour cream

DRESSING: In a small bowl, combine the dry mustard with ¼ teaspoon of the sugar and stir in 1 to 2 tablespoons of warm water, or enough to make a thick paste. Set aside for 15 minutes. Then stir in the sour cream and the remaining teaspoon of sugar.

SALAD

2 hard-cooked eggs, finely chopped

2 large or 4 small boiled and peeled fresh beets, or 4 canned beets, cut into ¼-inch dice

1 pound (about 3 medium) boiled potatoes, peeled and cut into ¼-inch dice

1 pound (about 2) sour dill pickles, cut lengthwise into narrow strips,

then crosswise into ⅛-inch-wide bits

1 fillet of pickled or *matjes* herring, drained and cut into ¼-inch dice

1 pound boiled beef, or cooked ham, veal or lamb, trimmed of fat and cut into ½-inch dice

1 large, tart red apple, cored, peeled and cut into ¼-inch dice

3 hard-cooked eggs, cut into quarters

SALAD: In a large mixing bowl, combine the finely chopped eggs, diced beets, potatoes, pickles, herring, meat and apple. Add the sour cream dressing and toss together lightly but thoroughly until all the ingredients are well moistened with the dressing.

Traditionally, *rossolye* is mounded high on a square or round serving plate, garnished with sliced hard-cooked eggs, and chilled. Serve as a first course or as part of a *zakuska* table.

Salat Olivier *(Russia)*

TART CHICKEN SALAD WITH SOUR-CREAM DRESSING

To serve 6

2 whole chicken breasts, about ¾ pound each
1 large onion, peeled and quartered
2 teaspoons salt
½ cup coarsely chopped, drained, sour dill pickles
4 boiled new potatoes, cooled, peeled, and thinly sliced
3 hard-cooked eggs, peeled and thinly sliced
⅛ teaspoon white pepper
¾ cup mayonnaise, freshly made or a good unsweetened commercial variety
¾ cup sour cream
2 tablespoons capers, drained, washed, and patted dry with paper towels
1 tablespoon finely cut fresh dill leaves
6 green olives
1 medium tomato, peeled *(see borshch ukraïnsky, page 21)* and cut lengthwise into eighths
1 small head Boston lettuce, the leaves separated, washed and dried with paper towels

In a heavy 2- to 3-quart pot, combine the chicken, onion and 1 teaspoon of the salt. Cover with about 1½ quarts of cold water and bring to a boil uncovered over high heat, skimming off the fat and scum as it rises to the surface. Partially cover the pan, reduce the heat to low, and simmer about 10 minutes, or until the chicken is tender. Remove the chicken from the pot and with a small, sharp knife, remove and discard the skin and cut the meat away from the bones. Cut the chicken meat into strips about ½ inch wide and combine them in a large mixing bowl with the pickles, potatoes and eggs. Sprinkle with the remaining teaspoon of salt and ⅛ teaspoon of white pepper. In a small bowl, beat together the mayonnaise and sour cream, and stir half of it into the salad. Taste for seasoning.

To serve *salat Olivier* in the traditional Russian manner, shape the salad into a pyramid in the middle of a serving platter. Mask with the remaining sour-cream-and-mayonnaise dressing and sprinkle it with capers and dill. Decorate with olives, tomatoes and lettuce leaves.

Agurkai su Rukcscia Grietne *(Baltic States)*
CUCUMBER-AND-SOUR-CREAM SALAD

To serve 4 to 6

4 medium cucumbers, peeled, halved, seeded, and cut crosswise into ½-inch-thick slices	1 tablespoon coarse salt, or substitute 2 tablespoons table salt ½ teaspoon white distilled vinegar

In a mixing bowl, combine the cucumber slices, salt and vinegar and toss them about with a large spoon until the cucumber is well moistened. Marinate at room temperature for 30 minutes, then drain the cucumbers through a sieve and pat them thoroughly dry with paper towels. Place them in a large mixing bowl.

DRESSING

3 hard-cooked eggs	⅛ teaspoon white pepper
1 teaspoon prepared mustard, preferably Dijon or Düsseldorf	
⅓ cup sour cream	4 to 6 large lettuce leaves, well washed and dried
2 teaspoons white wine vinegar	1 tablespoon finely cut fresh dill
¼ teaspoon sugar	leaves

Separate the yolks from the whites of the hard-cooked eggs. Cut the whites into strips ⅛ inch wide and 1 to 2 inches long and stir the egg whites into the cucumber.

With the back of a large spoon, rub the egg yolks through a fine sieve set over a small bowl. Slowly beat in the mustard, sour cream, white wine vinegar, sugar and white pepper. When the dressing is smooth, pour it over the cucumbers and toss together gently but thoroughly. Taste for seasoning.

To serve, arrange the lettuce leaves on a large flat serving plate or on small individual plates and mound the salad on top of them. Sprinkle with dill and refrigerate until ready to serve.

Mdzhavai Kombosto *(Caucasus)*
RED CABBAGE SALAD

This popular Georgian vegetable salad consists of white cabbage pickled in a marinade for several days until it turns red. Although it may appear more reasonable to make it with red cabbage, the piquant flavor given the white cabbage by its marinade will not be the same if you use the red variety.

To serve 4 to 6

A 2-pound white cabbage, trimmed and outer leaves removed	8 sprigs parsley, with stems cut off
2 pounds beets, peeled and cut into 1-inch dice	1 bunch celery, leaves only
	2 cups red wine vinegar
	1 teaspoon imported paprika

Place the cabbage in a 3- to 4-quart casserole and cover it with cold water. Bring to a boil over high heat, then reduce the heat to low and simmer, partially covered, for about 40 minutes, or until a knife inserted deeply into the cabbage meets only the slightest resistance.

With two slotted spoons, remove the cabbage from the water and place it in a colander to drain. Gently pull back the outer leaves, and carefully open and separate the inner leaves one by one without detaching them from their base. The cabbage should now have the shape of a large opened rose.

Set the cabbage in a deep 8- to 10-quart stainless-steel or enameled casserole. Add the beets, parsley, celery leaves, vinegar and paprika and pour in enough boiling water to cover the cabbage by at least 2 inches. Place a heavy heatproof plate on top of the cabbage to keep it submerged and pickle the cabbage at room temperature for 5 to 7 days. At the end of this period, it will have turned a deep, tawny red. Refrigerate it in its marinade for at least 4 hours before serving.

Remove the cabbage from its liquid, drain it thoroughly, and set it upright on a flat plate. Cut into quarters and serve.

NOTE: A simpler though less decorative way to prepare the salad is to chop the cooked cabbage coarsely before pickling it.

Marinovannye Griby *(Russia)*
PICKLED MUSHROOMS

To serve 6 to 8

1 cup red wine vinegar
2 whole cloves
½ cup cold water
5 whole black peppercorns
½ bay leaf

2 teaspoons salt
2 cloves garlic, peeled and crushed
   with the flat of a knife or cleaver
1 pound small, fresh white
   mushrooms
1 tablespoon vegetable oil

In a 1½- to 2-quart enameled or stainless-steel saucepan, combine the red wine vinegar, whole cloves, water, peppercorns, bay leaf, salt and crushed garlic. Bring to a boil over high heat, drop in the mushrooms, and reduce the heat to low. Simmer uncovered, for 10 minutes, stirring the mushrooms occasionally, then cool to room temperature.

Remove the garlic from the marinade and pour the entire contents of the pan into a 1-quart jar. Slowly pour the vegetable oil on top, secure the top with plastic wrap, and cover the jar tightly. Marinate the mushrooms in the refrigerator for at least one week.

Serve the pickled mushrooms as part of a *zakuska* table, or as a piquant accompaniment to meat or fish.

Bulviu Maltiniai *(Baltic States)*
FRIED POTATO PATTIES

To serve 8 to 10

3 pounds baking potatoes, peeled
   and quartered
1 egg

½ to ¾ cup flour
2 teaspoons salt

4 tablespoons butter for frying

Bring 4 quarts of water to a boil in a 6- to 8-quart pot and drop in the potatoes. Boil briskly, uncovered, until they are soft enough to be easily pierced with a fork. Drain them thoroughly in a large sieve and force them through a ricer or mash them in a bowl with a fork. Beat in the egg, ½ cup of flour and the salt, and continue to beat vigorously until the mixture is smooth and dense enough to hold its shape almost solidly in a spoon. (If the mixture seems too fluid, beat in the remaining flour, a tablespoon at a time.)

Gather the potato dough into a ball, place it on a heavily floured surface and pat it into a thick rectangle. With a floured rolling pin, roll it into a large rectangle about 1 inch thick, dusting it frequently with a little flour to prevent it from sticking to the pin or board. With a sharp knife or pastry wheel, cut 2-inch-wide strips down the length of the dough, then slice diagonally into 2½-inch-wide lengths. Gently score the top of each diamond-shaped patty by making shallow lines down its length.

Melt 2 tablespoons of the butter in a heavy 10- to 12-inch skillet set over high heat. When the foam has almost subsided add 6 or 8 of the patties and brown them 3 to 5 minutes on each side, turning them over carefully with a large spatula. Transfer the patties to a serving platter and cover them loosely with foil to keep them warm while you fry the remaining patties, adding more butter to the pan as needed.

Bulvių Vyniotinis su Mesa (*Baltic States*)
POTATO ROULADE FILLED WITH MEAT

To serve 8 to 10

	maltiniai, opposite)
1 recipe potato dough (*see bulvių*	Flour

Prepare the potato dough as described opposite, and gather it into a ball. On a sheet of lightly floured wax paper, roll the dough with a floured pin into a rectangle about 12 inches wide, 16 inches long and ½ inch thick.

STUFFING

1 pound boiled beef (*see shchi, page 20*), ground or finely chopped	½ teaspoon salt
	1 egg, lightly beaten
½ cup finely chopped onions	2 tablespoons dry bread crumbs
Freshly ground black pepper	2 teaspoons butter, softened

Preheat the oven to 400°. Combine the ground or chopped meat, onions, pepper and salt in a mixing bowl. Spread the meat mixture evenly over the entire surface of the potato dough. Starting with the wide side of the dough, lift the wax paper and using it to support the dough, roll the dough into a thick, compact cylinder. Brush the surface with the egg and sprinkle it evenly with bread crumbs.

With two large spatulas, transfer the roulade to a baking sheet lightly coated with 2 teaspoons of butter. Bake in the center of the oven for 30 minutes, or until the crust is golden brown. Slice the roulade crosswise into 2-inch-thick slices and serve at once.

Kugelis *(Baltic States)*
GRATED POTATO PUDDING

To serve 4

2 pounds boiling potatoes, peeled and coarsely grated	4 tablespoons clarified butter *(tabaka, page 55)*
1 whole egg	4 tablespoons butter
1 teaspoon salt	1 cup thinly sliced onions

Preheat the oven to 400°. In a large mixing bowl, combine the grated potatoes, egg and salt and mix together thoroughly. Pour the clarified butter
into a heavy 8-inch ovenproof pan. Add the potato mixture and smooth the
top with a rubber spatula. Bake uncovered for 20 minutes in the center of
the oven, or until the potatoes are golden brown and crusty. Place a flat
plate upside down on top of the pan and, grasping the plate and pan firmly together, invert them. The pudding should come out easily. Now carefully
slide the pudding back into the pan uncooked side up. Bake 20 minutes or
until the pudding is golden brown.

While the pudding is baking, melt the butter in a 10- to 12-inch skillet
over moderate heat. When the foam has almost subsided, add the sliced onions and, stirring frequently, cook them for 10 to 12 minutes, or until they
are soft and golden brown. Watch carefully for any sign of burning and regulate the heat accordingly.

Slide the potato pudding onto a heated serving platter and scatter the
onion rings over the top. Cut into pie-shaped wedges and serve at once.

Kartoplia Solimkoi *(Ukraine)*
DEEP-FRIED STRAW POTATOES

To serve 4 to 6

4 medium-sized baking potatoes (about 2 pounds)	Vegetable oil for deep-frying Salt

Peel the potatoes and cut them into straw-shaped strips, about 2½ inches
long and ⅛ inch thick. Drop them into a bowl of ice water and set them
aside until ready to fry. Drain the potatoes in a colander, spread them out
on a double thickness of paper towels and pat them thoroughly dry.

Pour enough oil into a deep fryer to come 3 or 4 inches up the sides of
the pan. For the first frying of the potatoes (there will be two in all), heat
the oil until it reaches a temperature of 370° on a deep-frying thermometer.

Drop the potatoes into the frying basket and immerse the basket in the hot oil, shaking it gently from time to time to prevent the potatoes from sticking together. Fry them for about 15 seconds, or until the potatoes are tender and a pale golden brown. Drain on a double thickness of paper towels, then fry and drain the remaining potatoes similarly. The potatoes may now rest for as long as an hour before refrying and serving.

Immediately before serving, reheat the oil until it reaches a temperature of 385° on a deep-frying thermometer. Drop all the potatoes into the basket and, shaking the basket occasionally, fry for 15 seconds, or until the potatoes are crisp and brown. Drain on paper towels and transfer to a large platter or bowl. Sprinkle lightly with salt, and serve at once.

Lokshyna, Zapechena z Syrom (Ukraine)
EGG NOODLE-AND-COTTAGE-CHEESE CASSEROLE

To serve 8

8 slices lean bacon	2 cups large-curd cottage cheese
3 cups cooked and drained egg	2 eggs
noodles *(page 36)*, or a good	¼ cup heavy cream
commercial variety	4 tablespoons unsalted butter
1½ teaspoons salt	½ cup fine dry bread crumbs

Fry the bacon in a 10- to 12-inch skillet until brown and crisp. Crumble it coarsely and combine it with its fat in a large mixing bowl. Add the cooked noodles, sprinkle with ½ teaspoon of the salt, and with two forks, toss together thoroughly. Place the cheese in a separate mixing bowl and beat in the eggs, the cream and the remaining teaspoon of salt.

Preheat the oven to 350°. With a pastry brush, lightly coat the bottom and sides of a 1½- to 2-quart baking dish with 1 tablespoon of the butter. Spread a layer of the noodles in the bottom of the dish. Top with half the cheese mixture, then repeat the layers, ending with a layer of noodles.

Melt the remaining 3 tablespoons of butter in a 10- to 12-inch skillet. Off the heat, stir the bread crumbs into the melted butter, then scatter the buttered crumbs over the top of the noodles. Bake in the center of the oven for about 30 minutes, or until the crumbs are golden brown. Serve at once.

Lokshyna Homen *(Ukraine)*
HOMEMADE EGG NOODLES

To make 3 cups

1 cup flour	3 to 4 teaspoons cold water
1 egg	¼ teaspoon salt

Pour the flour into a large mixing bowl, make a well in the center of the flour and add the egg, 3 teaspoons water and the salt. With a fork or your fingers gradually mix the flour into the liquid ingredients until the dough can be gathered into a rough ball. If the dough crumbles, add up to another teaspoon of water by drops until the particles adhere.

To make egg noodles by hand, knead the dough on a lightly floured board, kneading in a little extra flour if the dough seems sticky. In about 10 minutes, the dough should be shiny and elastic. Wrap it in wax paper and let it rest at room temperature for at least 10 minutes before rolling it.

Divide the dough in half. Place one half on a floured surface and flatten it with the palm of your hand into an oblong about 1 inch thick. Dust the dough lightly with flour, then roll it out lengthwise to within an inch of the farthest edges. Turn the dough crosswise and roll across its width. Repeat, turning and rolling the dough, until it is paper thin. If at any time the dough begins to stick, sprinkle a little more flour under and over it.

Dust the dough lightly with flour and let it dry for about 10 minutes. Then roll the dough into a thick compact cylinder. With a sharp knife, slice the roll crosswise into even strips ⅛ inch wide. Unroll the strips and set them aside on wax paper. Roll, shape and slice the second half of the dough similarly.

An Italian pasta machine will do both the kneading and rolling. Pull off about ⅓ of the dough, set the smooth rolls of the pasta machine as far apart as possible and feed the piece of dough through them. Reroll the strip four or five times, folding under the ragged edges and dusting the dough lightly with flour if it feels sticky. When the dough is smooth, shiny and elastic, it has been kneaded enough. To roll it out, set the machine at the second notch and feed the dough through with the rolls somewhat closer together than before. Then set the machine at the third notch and roll the dough thinner. Repeat, changing the notch after each rolling, until the dough is about 1/16 inch thick. Repeat this procedure with the remaining dough. Then cut the dough, sheet by sheet, into noodles by putting it through the ¼-inch cutting section.

Homemade egg noodles may be cooked at once, or wrapped securely in plastic wrap and refrigerated for as long as 24 hours. Cook them in 6 to 8 quarts of rapidly boiling water for 5 to 10 minutes, or until just tender but still slightly firm to the bite. Then drain thoroughly through a sieve or colander.

Lokshyna, Zapechena z Shpynatom *(Ukraine)*
EGG NOODLE-AND-SPINACH CASSEROLE

To serve 6 to 8

3 cups cooked and drained egg
  noodles *(opposite)*, or a
  good commercial variety
1½ tablespoons butter, melted
¾ cup finely grated Switzerland
  cheese
1 teaspoon salt
1 cup finely chopped onions
3 pounds fresh spinach, cooked,

squeezed and finely chopped, or
4 ten-ounce packages frozen
spinach, defrosted, squeezed
completely dry, and finely
chopped (about 3 cups)
6 tablespoons butter
Freshly ground black pepper
½ cup fine dry bread crumbs
4 hard-cooked eggs, quartered

In a large mixing bowl, toss the cooked noodles, melted butter, 6 tablespoons of the cheese and ½ teaspoon of the salt together with two forks.

Melt 3 tablespoons of the butter in a 10- to 12-inch enameled or stainless-steel skillet set over high heat. Add the chopped onions, reduce the heat to moderate, and cook 3 to 5 minutes, or until the onions are soft but not brown. Stir in the chopped spinach, raise the heat to high and, stirring constantly, cook uncovered until the moisture in the pan has completely evaporated and the spinach has begun to stick lightly to the pan. Stir in the remaining ½ teaspoon of salt and a few grindings of black pepper.

With a pastry brush, lightly coat the bottom and sides of a 1½- to 2-quart baking dish with 1 tablespoon of the butter. Arrange ⅓ of the noodles in a layer on the bottom of the dish and top with ½ the spinach. Repeat the layers, ending with noodles.

Melt the remaining 2 tablespoons of butter in a heavy skillet and, off the heat, stir in the bread crumbs and the remaining grated cheese. Sprinkle the crumb-and-cheese mixture on the top of the noodles and bake in the center of the oven for 30 minutes, or until the crumb-and-cheese topping is golden brown. Serve at once, garnished with the hard-cooked eggs.

Lobio *(Caucasus)*
RED BEANS WITH HERB DRESSING

To serve 4

½ cup dried red kidney beans, or substitute 1 cup canned red kidney beans	2 tablespoons finely chopped onions
	¼ cup finely chopped parsley
	¼ cup finely chopped fresh coriander
1½ teaspoons salt	Freshly ground black pepper
1 tablespoon white wine vinegar	2 tablespoons vegetable oil

If you are using the dried kidney beans, bring 4 cups of water and 1 teaspoon of the salt to a boil in a heavy 2- to 3-quart saucepan. Drop in the kidney beans and boil 2 minutes, then remove the pan from the heat and let the beans soak uncovered for 1 hour. Bring back to a boil, lower the heat and simmer uncovered for 1 hour, or until the beans are tender but still intact. Drain in a sieve or colander and pat dry with paper towels. Canned beans need only be drained, washed under cold running water and patted dry.

In a large bowl combine the vinegar, chopped onions, parsley, coriander, ½ teaspoon of salt, a generous grinding of black pepper and the oil. Mix thoroughly. Add the kidney beans, toss together gently but thoroughly with a fork and taste for seasoning. The beans may be served at once, but the flavor will be improved if they rest at room temperature for about 1 hour, stirring them from time to time.

Lobio Satsivi *(Caucasus)*
STRING BEANS IN WALNUT SAUCE

To serve 6 to 8

1 cup chicken stock, fresh or canned	3 tablespoons finely chopped fresh coriander *(cilantro)*
¼ cup finely chopped onions	
2 teaspoons finely chopped garlic	¼ pound walnuts, pulverized in a mortar and pestle, or ground in a nut grinder
2 teaspoons imported sweet paprika	
1½ teaspoons salt	
¼ cup red wine vinegar	1 pound fresh string beans, trimmed

In a large serving bowl combine the stock, onions, garlic, paprika, salt, vinegar, coriander and walnuts and mix together thoroughly.

Over high heat, bring 3 quarts of lightly salted water to a boil in a 4- to

5-quart pan. Drop in the string beans and boil them briskly, uncovered, for about 8 to 10 minutes, or until they are tender but still slightly resistant to the bite. Drain the beans in a colander, then add them to the walnut sauce. Toss together lightly but thoroughly, taste for seasoning and serve at once.

Lobio Tkemali *(Caucasus)*
RED BEANS WITH PLUM SAUCE

To serve 4 to 6

⅛ teaspoon finely chopped fresh basil, or substitute ¼ teaspoon crumbled dried basil
2 teaspoons finely chopped coriander *(cilantro)*, or substitute 3 teaspoons finely chopped Italian parsley
⅛ teaspoon cayenne pepper
¼ teaspoon salt

¼ teaspoon finely chopped garlic
3 tablespoons damson plum jam
½ teaspoon red wine vinegar
1 cup red kidney beans cooked and cooled *(see lobio, opposite)*, or substitute 2 cups canned red kidney beans, drained and washed under cold running water

Combine the basil, ½ teaspoon of the coriander or 1 teaspoon of the parsley, cayenne pepper, salt and garlic in a large bowl and mash to a paste with the back of a large wooden spoon.

Combine the jam and vinegar in a 1-quart enameled or stainless-steel saucepan and, stirring constantly, bring to a boil over high heat and continue to boil until the jam has dissolved. With the back of a wooden spoon, rub the mixture through a fine sieve set over a small bowl. Beat it into the herb-and-garlic paste, a tablespoon at a time. Add the beans and toss together gently until the beans are coated with the sauce. Taste for seasoning. Let the beans rest at room temperature for 2 or 3 hours, or cover with plastic wrap and refrigerate overnight. Serve the *lobio tkemali* at room temperature, sprinkled with the remaining chopped coriander or parsley.

Troskinti Raudoni Kapustai (Baltic States)
BRAISED RED CABBAGE WITH SOUR-CREAM SAUCE

To serve 6 to 8

A 3-pound red cabbage, cut into
    quarters, cored, then coarsely
    shredded
½ cup coarsely chopped onions
1 teaspoon finely chopped garlic
8 tablespoons tomato paste
1 cup cold water

1 teaspoon salt
6 tablespoons butter, cut into small
    pieces
1 teaspoon salt
3 tablespoons fresh lemon juice,
    strained
2 tablespoons sour cream

In a 4-quart enameled or stainless-steel casserole, combine the shredded cabbage, chopped onions and garlic. Mix the tomato paste in the water and stir into the cabbage. Add 1 teaspoon of the salt and the butter and, stirring constantly, bring to a boil over high heat. Then reduce the heat to low, cover the casserole and simmer 45 minutes, or until the cabbage is tender. Stir in the lemon juice and the remaining teaspoon of salt and remove from the heat. Stir in the sour cream and taste for seasoning. Serve directly from the casserole or mound the cabbage in the center of a large serving bowl. Braised cabbage makes an excellent accompaniment to chopped meat patties or stuffed shoulder of veal (page 60).

Karabakh Loby (Caucasus)
STRING BEANS IN SOUR CREAM AND TOMATO SAUCE

To serve 4 to 6

1 pound fresh string beans, trimmed
4 tablespoons butter
2 cups thinly sliced onions
1 small green pepper, seeded, deribbed
    and cut into ½-inch pieces
3 medium tomatoes, peeled, seeded
    and coarsely chopped (see borshch

ukraïnsky, page 21)
1 tablespoon finely chopped sweet,
    fresh basil leaves, or substitute
    1½ teaspoons dried crumbled basil
1 egg
1 cup sour cream
1 teaspoon salt
Freshly ground black pepper

In a 4- to 5-quart pan, bring 3 quarts of lightly salted water to a boil over high heat. Drop in the string beans a handful at a time and bring back to a boil. Lower the heat and cook uncovered for 8 to 10 minutes, or until the beans are tender but still slightly resistant to the bite. Drain the beans, wash them under cold running water and set aside.

Melt the butter in a heavy 10- to 12-inch skillet or 2-quart casserole set over high heat. Add the onions and green pepper, lower the heat and, stirring occasionally, cook 5 to 8 minutes, or until the vegetables are tender but not brown. Stir in the tomatoes and basil, raise the heat to high, and boil rapidly for 1 or 2 minutes, until most of the juices in the pan have evaporated. Stir in the green beans and simmer 1 or 2 minutes until heated through.

In a mixing bowl, beat together the egg, sour cream, salt and a few grindings of black pepper. Taste for seasoning and stir into the vegetables. Transfer to a serving bowl and serve at once.

Sabzi Piez *(Central Asia)*
BRAISED ONIONS AND CARROTS

To serve 4 to 6

3 tablespoons butter	strips (2 cups)
1 medium onion, thinly sliced and separated into rings (1 cup)	½ teaspoon salt
	⅛ teaspoon cayenne pepper
1 large tomato, peeled, seeded and finely chopped *(see borshch ukraïnsky, page 21)*	¼ cup finely chopped scallions, including 2 inches of the green stems
8 small carrots, scraped and sliced lengthwise into ⅛-inch-thick	2 tablespoons finely chopped fresh coriander *(cilantro)* or parsley

Melt the 3 tablespoons of butter in a heavy 10- to 12-inch stainless-steel or enameled skillet set over high heat. Drop in the onion rings and stirring frequently, cook over moderate heat for 8 to 10 minutes, or until they are golden brown. Add the tomatoes, raise the heat and boil briskly, uncovered, until most of the liquid in the pan has evaporated. Then stir in the carrots, salt and cayenne pepper.

Pour in just enough water (about ½ to ¾ cup) to barely cover the carrots, bring to a boil and cover the skillet tightly. Reduce the heat to low and simmer for about 10 minutes, or until the carrots are just tender. Transfer the carrots and the sauce to a heated serving bowl, sprinkle with chopped scallions and coriander or parsley, and serve at once.

FISH

Bitki s Zapravkoi Gorchichnoi (*Russia*)
FISH CAKES WITH MUSTARD SAUCE

To serve 4 to 6

MUSTARD SAUCE

2 tablespoons prepared mustard, preferably the Dijon or Düsseldorf variety
½ teaspoon salt
½ teaspoon pepper
1 teaspoon white wine vinegar

1 teaspoon fresh strained lemon juice
6 tablespoons vegetable oil
¼ cup finely chopped parsley
½ cup finely cut fresh dill leaves
2 teaspoons finely chopped sweet gherkins

Combine the mustard, salt and pepper in a small bowl. Add the vinegar and lemon juice and beat in the oil with a whisk until the mixture is smooth. Stir in the parsley, dill and chopped gherkins, cover with plastic wrap and refrigerate until ready to use.

FISH CAKES

8 slices homemade-type white bread, with crusts trimmed off
1 cup milk
2 pounds cod fillets, skinned and finely ground (2 cups)
¼ cup finely grated onion

¼ cup finely cut fresh dill leaves
2 teaspoons salt
¼ teaspoon white pepper
Flour
6 tablespoons butter
3 tablespoons vegetable oil

Soak the sliced bread in the milk for about 10 minutes, or until it has absorbed all of the milk. Squeeze it gently to rid it of any excess milk and mash it in a large bowl combining it with the ground fish, grated onion and dill. Season with salt and pepper and place the fish mixture on a floured surface. Shape the mixture into about 12 flat, round cakes 3 or 4 inches in diameter and about ½ inch thick.

Melt 4 tablespoons of the butter in a heavy 10- to 12-inch skillet and set over high heat. When the foam has begun to subside, drop in 4 to 6 of the fish cakes. Lower the heat to moderate and fry 2 or 3 minutes on each side, or until they are a golden brown. Transfer to a heated platter with a spatula, and cover loosely with foil to keep them warm while you fry the remaining fish cakes. Add the additional butter and oil to the pan as it is needed. Serve hot, accompanied by the mustard sauce.

Osetrina po-Russki *(Russia)*
STURGEON OR HALIBUT IN TOMATO AND MUSHROOM SAUCE

To serve 6 to 8

2 cups thinly sliced onions
1 bay leaf
¼ cup scraped, coarsely chopped carrots
½ cup scraped, coarsely chopped parsley root
4 medium tomatoes, peeled, seeded and coarsely chopped *(see borshch ukraïnsky, page 21)*

5 tablespoons unsalted butter
4 cups cold water
1½ pounds fresh sturgeon or halibut steaks
½ cup thinly sliced fresh mushrooms
½ cup heavy cream
1 tablespoon capers, drained and washed
¼ cup pitted green olives, washed under cold running water

Preheat the oven to 200°. In a 3- to 4-quart casserole, combine the onions, bay leaf, carrots, parsley root, tomatoes, 3 tablespoons of the butter and 4 cups of cold water. Bring to a boil over high heat, stirring constantly, then reduce the heat to moderate, partially cover the casserole, and simmer undisturbed for 30 minutes. Pour the entire contents of the casserole into a fine sieve set over a large bowl. Press down on the vegetables with the back of a large spoon to extract all their juices before discarding them.

Return the strained stock to the casserole, add the fish, and bring to a boil over high heat. Immediately reduce the heat to low, cover the casserole, and simmer 6 to 8 minutes, or until the fish is opaque and firm to the touch. Be careful not to overcook. With a wide spatula, transfer the fish to a deep ovenproof serving dish, cover it loosely with foil and keep it warm in the oven while you complete the sauce.

Again bring the stock to a boil over high heat, and continue to boil briskly, uncovered, until it has cooked down to about 1½ cups. Meanwhile, melt the 2 remaining tablespoons of butter in a 10- to 12-inch skillet over high heat, and when the foam has almost subsided, drop in the mushrooms. Reduce the heat to moderate and cook for 3 to 5 minutes, stirring the mushrooms occasionally, until they are soft and most of the juices have cooked away. Stir in the reduced stock and, off the heat, beat in the heavy cream, 1 tablespoon at a time. Then stir in the capers and olives and taste for seasoning. Pour the sauce over the fish and serve at once.

Osetrina Zalivnaya *(Russia)*

FISH IN ASPIC

To serve 6 to 8

FISH STOCK AND FISH
6 cups cold water
4 pounds fish trimmings: spines, heads and tails from any white-fleshed fish
2 medium carrots, scraped
4 sprigs parsley
2 stalks celery with leaves, coarsely chopped
¼ cup white wine vinegar
1 bay leaf
8 whole cloves
1 tablespoon salt
4 fresh sturgeon or halibut steaks, cut 1 inch thick and weighing about 8 ounces each

In a 2- to 3-quart enameled or stainless-steel casserole, combine 6 cups of cold water with the fish trimmings, carrots, parsley, celery, vinegar, bay leaf, cloves and salt. Bring to a boil over high heat, then reduce the heat to low and partially cover the pot. Simmer the stock undisturbed for 1 hour.

Remove the carrots with a slotted spoon and set them aside. Strain the stock through a fine sieve set over a 3- to 4-quart enameled or stainless-steel casserole, pressing down on the vegetables and trimmings with the back of a large spoon to extract all their juices before discarding them. Bring the stock to a boil over high heat and add the fish steaks. Cover the pot, reduce the heat to low, and simmer gently for 8 minutes, or until the fish is firm to the touch. Do not overcook. With a slotted spoon, transfer the fish to a platter and cut each steak in half.

There should be 4 cups of stock in the pot. If there is less, add cold water; if more, boil rapidly uncovered until it has reduced to 4 cups.

ASPIC
2 packages unflavored gelatin
½ cup water
4 egg whites

ASPIC: Pour the gelatin into the cold water and let it soften for 5 minutes. Meanwhile, beat the egg whites to a froth. Bring the stock to a boil over high heat and stir in the softened gelatin and egg whites. Stirring constantly with a whisk, boil until the aspic begins to froth and rise. When it almost threatens to overflow the pan remove it from the heat and let it rest for 5 minutes. Then pour the entire contents of the pan into a cheesecloth-lined sieve set over a deep bowl. Let the aspic drain through slowly without disturbing it at all. Discard the contents of the sieve and taste the aspic for seasoning. It should be quite definite in flavor and will doubtless need more salt.

Cut the carrots into ¼-inch slices and arrange them in concentric circles in the bottom of a 2-quart charlotte or a similar mold about 3 inches deep.

A teaspoon at a time, sprinkle the carrots evenly with the aspic and continue adding the aspic by the teaspoon until the carrots are half submerged, but not floating in the liquid. Place the mold in the refrigerator without dislodging the design and chill for at least 1 hour, or until the aspic is firm. By this time, the remaining aspic should be cool. Arrange half of the fish in a single layer on the aspic in the mold and pour in just enough aspic to submerge them. Refrigerate for at least 1 hour, or until the aspic is firm, then arrange the remaining fish on top and cover with the remaining aspic. Refrigerate for 2 hours, or until firm.

To unmold the aspic, run a sharp knife around the sides of the dish and dip the bottom in hot water for a few seconds. Place a flat, shallow platter upside down over the dish and, grasping both firmly together, invert the two. Rap the platter on a table and the aspic should slide out easily. Serve as a first course or a light luncheon dish, or as part of a *zakuska* table.

Tarti Champorzeh Shamtsuari (*Caucasus*)
STURGEON OR SWORDFISH ON SKEWERS

To serve 4

¼ cup fresh strained lemon juice	GARNISH
¼ cup sour cream	1 lemon, quartered
2 pounds sturgeon or swordfish, cut into 1½-inch cubes	8 to 10 scallions, trimmed, thoroughly washed and dried
1 tablespoon salt	2 medium, firm, ripe tomatoes,
2 tablespoons butter, melted	quartered

Light a layer of coals in a charcoal broiler and burn until a white ash appears on the surface; or preheat your kitchen broiler to its highest point.

In a large mixing bowl, combine the lemon juice and sour cream and mix thoroughly. Sprinkle the fish with the salt, then with a pastry brush, coat both sides of the fish with the sauce. Thread the cubes lengthwise on 4 skewers, pressing them firmly together.

Broil 4 inches from the source of the heat, basting the cubes from time to time with the melted butter. Turn the fish over after 4 minutes, brush with the remaining sour-cream mixture and broil another 2 to 3 minutes, or until the fish is golden brown and firm to the touch. Serve at once, accompanied by the quartered lemon, scallions and tomatoes.

Marinuota Silke *(Baltic States)*

FISH IN TOMATO MARINADE

To serve 6

MARINADE	1 teaspoon sugar
¾ cup vegetable oil	¼ teaspoon powdered cloves
2 cups coarsely chopped onions	1 bay leaf, coarsely crumbled
¾ cup tomato paste (6 ounces)	5 whole black peppercorns
3 tablespoons white distilled vinegar	1 teaspoon salt

MARINADE: In a heavy 10- to 12-inch skillet, heat the oil over high heat until a light haze forms above it. Drop in the onions, reduce the heat to moderate and, stirring frequently, cook for 8 to 10 minutes, or until the onions are soft but not brown. Stir in the tomato paste, vinegar, sugar, cloves, bay leaf, peppercorns and salt and bring to a boil. Cover the pan, reduce the heat to low, and simmer undisturbed for about 15 minutes. Then remove from the heat and cool the marinade to lukewarm.

1 ½ pounds whitefish fillets with skin left on, cut into 2-inch pieces, or 6 *schmaltz* herring fillets, soaked in cold water for 12 hours, cut into 2-inch pieces and patted dry with	paper towels 1 tablespoon salt Freshly ground black pepper ½ cup flour ½ cup vegetable oil

FISH: If you are using the whitefish, sprinkle it with the tablespoon of salt and a few grindings of pepper. Because they are quite salty to begin with, the herring pieces need only be sprinkled with pepper. Whatever the fish, coat it well with the flour and vigorously shake off any excess.

In a heavy 10- to 12-inch skillet, heat ½ cup of oil over high heat until a light haze forms above it. Add 6 or 8 pieces of the fish, lower the heat to moderate, and brown them 3 to 5 minutes on each side, turning the pieces over with tongs. Transfer the browned fish with tongs to a double thickness of paper towels to drain, and fry and drain the remaining fish similarly.

Pour ⅓ of the marinade into a shallow 2-quart enameled, glass or stainless-steel baking dish and arrange half the fish in it in one layer. Moisten the fish with ⅓ more of the marinade and arrange the remaining fish in another layer on top. Pour in the remaining marinade and let the fish marinate uncovered and unrefrigerated for at least 6 hours. Then refrigerate, tightly covered with plastic wrap, for at least 24 hours before serving. The herring will keep as long as 1 week in the refrigerator; in fact, its flavor will improve with longer marination.

GARNISH

2 tablespoons finely chopped parsley   1 hard-cooked egg, finely chopped

To serve, transfer the fish to a serving platter, moisten it with a little of the marinade if you like, and sprinkle with the parsley and hard-cooked eggs.

Silke Cepts ar Sipoli Merce *(Baltic States)*
FRIED HERRING WITH ONION SAUCE

To serve 2 to 4

2 fillets *schmaltz* herring (½ pound),   ½ cup flour
   or substitute 2 fillets pickled herring   2 tablespoons vegetable oil

Dip the herring fillets into the flour, coating them well on both sides. Then shake them vigorously to rid them of any excess flour. In a heavy 10- to 12-inch skillet, heat the oil over high heat until a light haze forms above it. Drop in the herring and fry about 2 minutes on each side, turning them over carefully with a large spatula. When they are golden brown on both sides, transfer them to a heated serving plate and cover them loosely with foil to keep them warm while you make the sauce.

SAUCE   ¼ cup sour cream
2 tablespoons butter   ¼ teaspoon salt
6 tablespoons finely chopped onions   Freshly ground black pepper
½ teaspoon flour   ¼-½ teaspoon fresh strained lemon
1 teaspoon prepared mustard   juice

In the same skillet, melt 2 tablespoons of butter over moderate heat. Add the chopped onions and, stirring frequently, cook for about 5 minutes, or until they are soft but not brown. Stir in the flour, then the mustard, sour cream, salt and a few grindings of pepper. Stirring constantly, simmer over low heat for about a minute, or until the sauce thickens lightly. Off the heat, stir in the lemon juice and taste for seasoning. Pour the sauce into a small bowl or sauceboat and serve at once with the herring as a first course or as part of a *zakuska* table.

POULTRY

Kurnik *(Russia)*
CHICKEN AND RICE PIE

To serve 8 to 10

PASTRY DOUGH
12 tablespoons chilled butter, cut into ¼-inch bits
4 tablespoons chilled vegetable

shortening
3 cups all-purpose flour
½ teaspoon salt
7 to 10 tablespoons ice water

PASTRY DOUGH: In a large chilled mixing bowl, combine the butter, vegetable shortening, flour and salt. Working quickly, use your fingertips to rub the flour and fat together until they blend and look like flakes of coarse meal. Pour 7 tablespoons of ice water over the mixture all at once, toss together lightly and gather the dough into a ball. If it crumbles, add up to 3 more tablespoons of ice water by drops until the particles adhere. Dust the pastry lightly with flour and wrap in wax paper. Refrigerate for at least 2 hours, or until firm.

FILLING
2 medium onions, peeled
1 stalk celery with leaves
1 large clove garlic, peeled
6 whole black peppercorns
2 whole cloves
1 large bay leaf
1½ teaspoons salt
A 4-pound stewing fowl, cut into quarters
The giblets of the fowl, coarsely chopped
8 tablespoons butter (¼ pound stick)

1 pound fresh mushrooms, thinly sliced
2 tablespoons finely chopped parsley
1 teaspoon fresh strained lemon juice
¼ teaspoon ground nutmeg
½ cup heavy cream
1 cup unconverted long-grain white rice
3 cups thinly sliced onions
5 hard-cooked eggs, finely chopped
¼ cup finely cut fresh dill leaves
2 tablespoons butter softened
1 egg yolk, dissolved in 2 tablespoons cream

FILLING: In a heavy 6- to 8-quart enameled or stainless-steel casserole, combine the onions, celery, garlic, peppercorns, cloves, bay leaf, salt, fowl and giblets and pour in enough cold water to cover the chicken by about 1 inch. Bring to a boil over high heat, meanwhile skimming off all the foam and scum with a large spoon as they rise to the surface. Then reduce the heat to low and simmer partially covered for 1½ hours, or until the fowl is tender but not falling apart.

Transfer the bird to a large platter and strain the stock through a fine sieve set over a bowl, pressing down hard on the herbs and vegetables with the back of a spoon before discarding them. Set the stock aside. With a small, sharp knife, remove the skin from the chicken and cut the meat away from the bones. Discard the skin and bones, cut the meat into 1-inch pieces and return them to the casserole.

In a 10- to 12-inch enameled or stainless-steel skillet, melt 4 tablespoons of the butter over high heat. Add the sliced mushrooms, reduce the heat to moderate and cook 3 to 5 minutes, or until the mushrooms are soft. With a slotted spoon, transfer them to the chicken in the casserole. Add the chopped parsley, lemon juice, nutmeg, cream and ½ cup of the reserved stock. Stir together thoroughly, taste for seasoning and set aside.

Combine the rice and 2 cups of the reserved stock in a 1½- to 2-quart saucepan. Bring to a boil over high heat, stirring occasionally, then cover the pan, lower the heat, and simmer for 15 to 18 minutes, or until the rice has absorbed all the stock. Set aside off the heat.

In the large skillet, melt the remaining 4 tablespoons of butter over high heat. Add the sliced onions, lower the heat and cook 10 to 15 minutes, or until the onions are soft and golden. Stir the onions into the rice and toss together until well combined.

In a separate bowl combine the chopped eggs and dill.

Preheat the oven to 400°. With a pastry brush and the 2 tablespoons of softened butter, lightly coat the bottom and sides of a baking dish about 9 by 12 inches and 2 inches deep. Spread ⅓ of the rice mixture on the bottom of the dish and cover with ½ the chicken mixture. Top the chicken with ½ the eggs and dill and repeat the layers, ending with a layer of rice.

On a lightly floured surface, roll the dough into a ⅛-inch-thick rectangle about 10 inches wide, and 14 inches long. Drape the pastry over the rolling pin, lift it up and unfold it slackly over the pan. Firmly press the edges of the pastry against the sides of the dish, pinching the edges to seal them. With a small, sharp knife, cut out a 1-inch circle from the middle of the dough. Brush the pastry with the egg yolk-and-cream mixture and bake in the center of the oven for 15 minutes. Reduce the temperature to 350° and bake an additional 30 to 40 minutes, or until the crust is golden brown. Serve at once.

Kotlety po-kyivskomu *(Ukraine)*
DEEP-FRIED CHICKEN CUTLETS WRAPPED AROUND BUTTER (CHICKEN KIEV)

Chicken Kiev is one of the great classic Ukraine dishes that has achieved international fame. The traditional Ukrainian recipe calls for boned pounded chicken breasts —fresh, never frozen—rolled around fingers of unseasoned butter. Less traditional are the herb seasonings suggested below, which add a note of interest to an otherwise bland, though typical, dish.

To serve 4

4 whole fresh chicken breasts, ½ to ¾ pound each, with or without the wing bone attached	OPTIONAL SEASONINGS
	1 teaspoon fresh, strained lemon juice
12 tablespoons chilled unsalted butter (1½ sticks)	1 teaspoon finely cut fresh chives or tarragon
2 eggs	1 tablespoon finely chopped parsley
Flour	
2 cups fine, dry white bread crumbs	2 teaspoons salt
Vegetable oil for deep-frying	Freshly ground black pepper

To skin the chicken breasts, start at the pointed end of the breast, insert your thumb under the skin, and strip it off. Bone and halve the breasts as described in the diagram at the top of page 138 in the main book. To prepare the chicken breasts with the wing bone attached, cut off the wing tip and its adjacent bone and leave only the short leglike bone attached to each breast.

Place the 8 halved breasts smooth-side down on a cutting board. With a small, sharp knife and your fingers, remove the small fillet from each breast. Lay the breasts and fillets, one pair at a time, on a sheet of wax paper. Cover the breast and fillet with a sheet of wax paper and, with the flat side of a cleaver or a metal meat pounder, pound them to a thickness of ⅛ inch. If holes appear in the flesh, overlap the edges of the tear slightly, cover the patch with wax paper, and pound gently until the meat joins together.

Cut the 1½ sticks of butter into 8 equal parts. Shape each piece of butter into a cylinder about ½ inch thick and 3 inches long. Wrap them in wax paper and chill until firm. (Or, cream the butter by mashing it against the side of a bowl with a wooden spoon. Beat into it all the optional seasonings and cut and shape the butter as described above. Chill until firm.)

To assemble the cutlets, gently peel off the wax paper and sprinkle the chicken lightly with salt and freshly ground black pepper. Wrap the chicken breasts and fillets around the butter fingers as shown on pages 138-139 in the main book.

In a small bowl, beat the eggs just long enough to combine them. Spread flour and the bread crumbs on two separate strips of wax paper and, one at a

50

time, dip the cutlets into the flour. Shake each one gently free of excess flour and, cradling it in your palms, pat the cutlet into a long cylinder tapering slightly at each end. Now dip the cutlet into the eggs, making sure its entire surface is coated, and roll in the bread crumbs, again making sure it is thoroughly coated. Arrange the cutlets side by side on a platter and refrigerate for 1 or 2 hours before frying.

About 30 minutes before you plan to serve the chicken, preheat the oven to 200°. Line a shallow baking dish with a double thickness of paper towels and place it in the oven. Pour enough oil to rise 3 or 4 inches up the side of a deep-fat fryer or a heavy saucepan into which a frying basket will fit. Set the pan over high heat until the oil registers 360° on a deep-fat thermometer. Fry the cutlets, 4 at a time, in the frying basket for about 5 minutes, or until golden brown, then transfer them with tongs or a slotted spoon to the lined baking dish. Fry the remaining cutlets similarly. The finished cutlets may remain in the low oven for no longer than 10 minutes before serving or they will lose their freshness and their butter may escape.

Traditionally, chicken Kiev is served accompanied by peas and by *kasha* or straw potatoes *(Recipe Index)*.

Tkemali *(Caucasus)*
SOUR PRUNE SAUCE

To make 1½ cups

	coriander *(cilantro)*
2 cups water	¼ teaspoon salt
½ pound sour prunes (about 24)	⅛ teaspoon cayenne pepper
1 clove garlic, peeled	2 tablespoons strained fresh lemon
3 tablespoons finely chopped	juice

Bring the 2 cups of water to a boil in a 1-quart saucepan and drop in the prunes. Remove from the heat and set aside for 10 minutes, then bring the water back to a boil over high heat. Cook briskly uncovered for 10 to 15 minutes, or until the prunes are tender. Pour the contents of the pan into a sieve set over a small bowl and set the liquid aside.

With a small, sharp knife cut out and discard the prune pits and combine the prunes, garlic and coriander in an electric blender. Pour in ¼ cup of the reserved prune liquid and blend at high speed, gradually adding the remaining prune liquid. The blended sauce should have the consistency of sour cream.

With a rubber spatula, transfer the sauce to a 1½- to 2-quart saucepan and stir in the salt and pepper. Bring to a boil over high heat, then, off the heat, stir in the lemon juice. Cool to room temperature and serve with *shashlyk* or *tabaka (Recipe Index)*.

Tushenaia Kuritsa Pod Sousom iz Chernosliv *(Russia)*

BRAISED CHICKEN WITH PRUNE SAUCE

To serve 4

A 2½- to 3-pound chicken, quartered
1 tablespoon salt
Freshly ground black pepper
4 tablespoons butter
2 tablespoons vegetable oil
1 carrot, scraped and cut into
 ½-inch-wide rounds
1 stalk celery, coarsely chopped
1 cup finely chopped onions

1 sprig parsley
1 bay leaf
½ to 1 cup chicken stock, fresh or
 canned
1½ cups water
½ pound pitted prunes
1 tablespoon fresh strained lemon
 juice
1 tablespoon sugar
1 tablespoon flour

Pat the chicken thoroughly dry with paper towels, and sprinkle it on all sides with the tablespoon of salt and a few grindings of pepper. In a heavy 10-to 12-inch enameled or stainless-steel skillet, melt 2 tablespoons of the butter in the 2 tablespoons of oil over high heat. When the foam begins to subside, add the chicken skin-side down. Reduce the heat to moderate and fry 5 to 6 minutes on each side, or until golden brown. Transfer the chicken quarters to a plate. Add the carrot, celery and onions to the fat remaining in the pan and, stirring occasionally, cook over moderate heat for about 5 minutes, or until the vegetables are soft but not brown. Return the chicken to the pan, lay the parsley and bay leaf on top and pour in ½ cup of chicken stock. Cover tightly and bring to a boil over high heat. Then lower the heat and simmer the chicken (basting it from time to time with the juices in the pan) for about 30 minutes, or until its juices run yellow when a thigh is pierced with the tip of a small, sharp knife.

Meanwhile, in a 1-quart enameled or stainless-steel saucepan, combine the 1½ cups water, prunes, lemon juice and sugar. Bring to a boil over high heat, then lower the heat and simmer uncovered for about 30 minutes, or until the prunes are tender. Set the prunes and their cooking liquid aside.

Preheat the oven to 250°. Remove the chicken from the skillet and arrange the pieces attractively on a large, heated, ovenproof platter. Scatter the cooked prunes over the top, cover loosely with foil and keep warm in the oven while you make the sauce.

Strain the contents of the skillet through a fine sieve set over a small saucepan, pressing down hard on the vegetables with the back of a spoon before discarding them. Set the juices aside.

Melt the remaining 2 tablespoons of butter in the skillet and stir in the flour. Cook for 2 or 3 minutes, stirring constantly, until the flour turns lightly brown. Pour in ½ cup of the reserved prune juice and ½ cup of the reserved pan juices (if there is less, augment it with chicken stock) and stirring constantly, bring to a boil. Boil until the sauce is smooth and has thickened lightly. Taste for seasoning and pour over the chicken. Serve at once.

Kotlety Pozharskie *(Russia)*
GROUND CHICKEN CUTLETS

To make 6 cutlets

4 ounces homemade-style white bread, trimmed of crusts (5 slices)
¼ cup milk
2 whole chicken breasts (about 2 pounds), skinned and boned *(see drawings, page 138, main book)*, or substitute 1 whole chicken breast, skinned and boned, and 1 pound finely ground lean veal

8 tablespoons unsalted butter, softened (¼-pound stick)
¾ teaspoon salt
¼ teaspoon white pepper
2 cups fresh bread crumbs made from homemade-style white bread, pulverized in a blender or shredded with a fork
10 tablespoons unsalted butter, cut into small bits

In a small bowl combine the 5 slices of bread and ¼ cup of milk. Soak the bread for about 15 minutes, then squeeze the bread dry with your fingers.

Cut the chicken into small pieces and grind them through the finest blades of the meat grinder twice. Combine the purée with the soaked bread and grind again (with the veal, if you plan to use it). With a large spoon, gradually beat in the 8 tablespoons of softened butter, salt and pepper and continue to beat until the mixture is smooth. Dip your fingers into cold water and shape the mixture into 6 oval patties, each about 1½ inches thick. Roll the patties in the bread crumbs, coating them thoroughly.

Clarify the 10 tablespoons of butter in the following fashion: Melt it slowly in a heavy 10- to 12-inch skillet set over low heat without letting it brown, skimming off the foam with a large spoon as it rises. Remove the pan carefully from the heat, let it rest for 2 or 3 minutes, then spoon off the clear butter and discard the milky solids (whey) at the bottom of the pan. Return 6 tablespoons of the butter to the pan. Place over moderately high heat and when the butter is very hot, add the patties. Fry about 5 minutes on each side, turning them over with a spatula. The patties are done when their outside crusts are golden brown and the purée inside shows no trace of pink when pierced with the tip of a sharp knife. Serve at once, and pour the remaining clarified butter evenly over them.

Kotmis Satsivi *(Caucasus)*

ROAST CHICKEN WITH WALNUT SAUCE

To serve 4

ROAST CHICKEN
A 3- to 3 1/2-pound chicken
4 tablespoons melted butter

1 tablespoon vegetable oil
1/2 teaspoon salt
Freshly ground black pepper

Pat the chicken dry inside and out with paper towels, then truss it securely with white kitchen cord. Mix the melted butter and vegetable oil together and with a pastry brush, coat the chicken thoroughly.

Preheat the oven to 475°. In a shallow roasting pan just large enough to hold the chicken comfortably, set it on its side on a rack. Roast in the center of the oven for about 10 minutes, then turn it on its other side. With a pastry brush, baste it with the butter-oil mixture and again roast 10 minutes. Now turn the chicken on its back and lower the heat to 400°. Baste again, sprinkle the bird with the salt and a few grindings of pepper and roast 40 minutes longer, basting every 10 minutes with the remaining butter-oil mixture and then with the juices in the pan. To test for doneness, pierce the thigh of the bird with the tip of a sharp knife. The juice that trickles out should be yellow; if it is pink, roast the bird for another 5 or 10 minutes.

WALNUT SAUCE
2 tablespoons butter
2 tablespoons finely chopped onions
2 teaspoons finely chopped garlic
1 tablespoon flour
1 1/2 cups chicken stock, fresh or
  canned
2 tablespoons red wine vinegar
1/8 teaspoon powdered cloves

1/8 teaspoon cinnamon
1/8 teaspoon cayenne
1 small bay leaf
1/8 teaspoon powdered saffron
1 tablespoon finely chopped parsley
1/4 teaspoon salt
3 ounces shelled walnuts, pulverized
  with a mortar and pestle or with
  a nut grinder

While the chicken is roasting prepare the sauce. In a heavy 10- to 12-inch skillet, melt 2 tablespoons of butter over high heat. Add the chopped onions and garlic, lower the heat and, stirring occasionally, cook uncovered for 3 to 5 minutes, or until the onions are soft but not brown. Stir in the flour, mix to a paste, then pour in the chicken stock. Bring to a boil over high heat, stirring constantly until the sauce thickens lightly. Stir in the vinegar, cloves, cinnamon, cayenne, bay leaf, saffron, parsley, salt and walnuts. Lower the heat and simmer uncovered for about 5 minutes. Taste for seasoning.

Carve the chicken into quarters and arrange them attractively on a deep serving platter. Pour the *satsivi* sauce over the chicken and serve at once.

Tabaka *(Caucasus)*

PRESSED FRIED CHICKEN

Georgians prepare small chickens in this unusual fashion—the backbone removed, the chicken flattened and then fried under a weight—so that the birds brown and cook quickly, and retain their shape.

To serve 4

4 squab chickens (1 to 1¼ pounds each)	4 tablespoons sour cream
	6 tablespoons butter, clarified *(below)*
Salt	1 cup *tkemali* sauce *(page 51)*

Pat the chickens thoroughly dry with paper towels. Following the illustrations on page 170 in the main book, remove the backbone, flatten the chickens, and draw their legs up through slits in the breasts.

Clarify the 6 tablespoons of butter in the following fashion: Melt it slowly in a heavy 10- to 12-inch skillet set over low heat, without letting it brown. Skim off the foam with a large spoon as it rises to the surface. Remove the pan carefully from the heat, let it rest 2 or 3 minutes, then spoon off the clear butter and discard the milky solids (whey) at the bottom of the pan.

Preheat the oven to 250°. Sprinkle both sides of the chickens liberally with salt and spread the flesh sides evenly with half the sour cream. Pour 2 tablespoons of the clarified butter into a heavy 10- to 12-inch skillet set over high heat and when the butter begins to brown, place 2 of the chickens skin-side down in the pan. Set a heavy weight—such as another skillet laden with cans of food—on top of the chickens, reduce the heat to moderate, and fry for 8 to 10 minutes. Then turn the chickens over with tongs, brush them with half of the remaining sour cream, and fry—again under the weight —for 10 minutes, or until they are a deep golden brown. Watch for any sign of burning, and regulate the heat accordingly.

When the chickens are done, place them skin-side up on an ovenproof platter. Keep them warm in the oven while you add the remaining butter to the skillet and proceed to fry the other chickens as before. Serve 1 whole chicken per person, accompanied by a bowl of *tkemali* sauce.

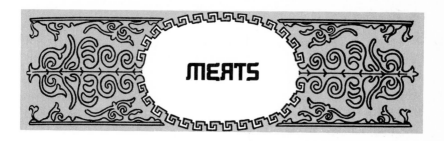

MEATS

Basturma *(Caucasus)*

MARINATED SKEWERED BEEF

To serve 4

¼ cup finely grated onion
2 tablespoons finely cut fresh basil,
   or substitute 1 tablespoon dried
   crumbled basil
½ teaspoon salt

⅛ teaspoon freshly ground black
   pepper
¼ cup red wine vinegar
2 pounds beef fillet or boneless
   sirloin, cut into 1½-inch cubes

In a large mixing bowl, combine the grated onion, basil, salt, pepper and vinegar. Add the meat and toss it in the marinade to coat it thoroughly, then marinate at room temperature for 5 to 6 hours. Toss the cubes about in the marinade every hour or so to keep them well moistened.

   Light a layer of coals in a charcoal broiler and burn until a white ash appears on the surface, or preheat your kitchen broiler to its highest point.

GARNISH

6 to 8 scallions, cut into 4-inch
   lengths, washed thoroughly and
   dried

1 lemon, quartered
Fresh coriander *(cilantro)* or parsley
   sprigs

   Remove the meat from the marinade and string the cubes on 4 long skewers, pressing them firmly together. Broil 4 inches from the source of the heat, turning the skewers occasionally, until the meat is done to your taste. For rare meat, allow about 10 minutes in all; well-done meat will take about 15 minutes. Slide the meat off the skewers onto heated individual plates and garnish with the scallions, quartered lemon and coriander or parsley sprigs.

Bef Stroganov *(Russia)*

SAUTÉED BEEF WITH MUSHROOMS AND ONIONS IN SOUR-CREAM SAUCE

Created in the late 19th Century for a Russian count, "bef Stroganov" has become one of the world's famous dishes. The recipe that follows is the classic Russian version. The numerous European and American variations called beef Stroganov do not in any sense reproduce the dish as it was originally made.

To serve 4 to 6

1 tablespoon powdered mustard	1 pound fresh mushrooms, thinly sliced lengthwise
1 tablespoon sugar	2 pounds fillet of beef, trimmed of all fat
2 teaspoons salt	1 teaspoon freshly ground black pepper
4 to 5 tablespoons vegetable oil	1 pint sour cream
4 cups thinly sliced onions separated into rings	

In a small bowl combine the mustard, 1½ teaspoons of the sugar, a pinch of the salt and enough hot water (perhaps a tablespoon) to form a thick paste. Let the mustard rest at room temperature for about 15 minutes.

Heat 2 tablespoons of the oil in a heavy 10- to 12-inch skillet over high heat until a light haze forms above it. Drop in the onions and mushrooms, cover the pan, and reduce the heat to low. Stirring from time to time, simmer 20 to 30 minutes, or until the vegetables are soft. Drain them in a sieve, discard the liquid and return the mixture to the skillet.

With a large, sharp knife cut the fillet across the grain into ¼-inch-wide rounds. Lay each round on a board and slice it with the grain into ¼-inch-wide strips. Heat 2 tablespoons of oil in another heavy 10- to 12-inch skillet over high heat until very hot but not smoking. Drop in half the meat and, tossing the strips constantly with a large spoon, fry for 2 minutes or so until the meat is lightly browned. With a slotted spoon transfer the meat to the vegetables in the other skillet and fry the remaining meat similarly, adding additional oil if necessary. When all the meat has been combined with the vegetables, stir in the remaining salt, pepper and the mustard paste. Stir in the sour cream, a tablespoon at a time, then add the remaining ½ teaspoon of sugar and reduce the heat to low. Cover the pan and simmer 2 or 3 minutes, or until the sauce is heated through. Taste for seasoning.

To serve *bef Stroganov*, transfer the contents of the pan to a heated serving platter and, if you like, scatter straw potatoes *(Recipe Index)* over the top.

Sult (*Baltic States*)

JELLIED VEAL

To serve 6 to 8

1½ pounds shoulder of veal cut into 2-inch pieces
1½ pounds fresh pig's knuckles, cracked with a cleaver
1 large onion (about 1 pound), unpeeled
1 large carrot, scraped and cut crosswise into ⅛-inch-thick rounds
2 quarts cold water
6 whole black peppercorns
3 bay leaves
1 tablespoon salt
1 teaspoon finely chopped garlic

In a heavy 4- to 6-quart casserole, combine the veal, pig's knuckles, onion, carrot, and water and bring to a boil over high heat, meanwhile skimming the foam and scum from the surface as they rise to the top. Then add the whole peppercorns and bay leaves, reduce the heat to low, and simmer partially covered for about 3 hours, or until the veal is tender enough to be easily pierced with a fork.

With a slotted spatula, transfer the veal and pig's knuckle to a plate. Strain the cooking stock in the casserole through a fine sieve set over a large bowl and let it rest for about 10 minutes. Then with a large spoon, skim off and discard all the surface fat. Pour the stock into a small pan and boil it briskly, uncovered, until it has cooked down to 4 cups.

When the veal and pig's knuckle are cool enough to handle, trim off the fat with a small knife and cut the meat away from the bones. Discard the bones and cut the meat into ¼-inch-wide shreds.

Arrange the carrot slices in concentric circles in the bottom of a 2-quart charlotte or a similar mold at least 3 inches deep. A teaspoon at a time, sprinkle the carrots evenly with the stock, and continue adding the stock by teaspoons until the carrots are half submerged but not floating in the liquid. Carefully place the mold in the refrigerator without dislodging the design and chill for at least 1 hour, or until the stock has firmly jelled.

By this time the remaining stock should be cool. Stir in the meat, salt and garlic and taste for seasoning. Then pour the entire mixture into the chilled mold. Refrigerate for at least 4 hours, or until the stock is firm.

To unmold, run a knife around the inside edges of the jellied veal. Dip the bottom of the mold briefly in hot water, then invert a flat serving dish on top. Holding mold and plate firmly together, turn them over. The jellied veal should slide out easily. Traditionally, *sult* is served as a first course or on the *zakuska* table.

Teliatyna z Pidlyvoiu iz Ikry (Ukraine)
BRAISED VEAL WITH CAVIAR SAUCE

To serve 6 to 8

3 tablespoons butter	3 tablespoons vegetable oil
1 cup thinly sliced onions	3½- to 4-pound boneless veal, cut
1 carrot, scraped and cut into ½-inch rounds	from either the leg or the rump and securely tied
4 sprigs parsley	1 cup dry white wine
2 stalks celery with their leaves, cut into 2-inch lengths	Salt
	Freshly ground black pepper
3 bay leaves	2 teaspoons potato starch dissolved
3 whole cloves	in 2 tablespoons cold water
1 tablespoon finely chopped lemon peel	2 tablespoons (1 ounce) black caviar
	⅛ teaspoon fresh lemon juice

In a heavy 6-quart casserole, melt the butter over high heat. Add the onions, carrot, parsley, celery, bay leaves, cloves and lemon peel and cover the pan. Lower the heat and simmer for about 15 minutes, until the vegetables are soft but not brown. Set aside.

Preheat the oven to 325°. In a heavy 10- to 12-inch skillet, heat the 3 tablespoons of oil over high heat until a light haze forms above it. Add the veal and brown for 8 to 10 minutes, turning it every 2 or 3 minutes so that it browns evenly on all sides. Then place it on top of the vegetables in the casserole and pour in the wine. Bring to a boil over high heat, sprinkle the meat liberally with salt and a few grindings of black pepper and cover the casserole tightly. Braise in the center of the oven for 1¼ hours, turning the veal over after 45 minutes.

When the veal is tender, transfer it to a heated platter, cut away the strings and carve the meat into ¼-inch-thick slices. Arrange them, slightly overlapping, down the center of a large platter and cover the platter loosely with foil to keep the meat warm while you make the sauce.

Quickly strain the entire contents of the casserole through a fine sieve into a bowl, pressing down hard on the vegetables with the back of a large spoon before discarding them. Skim off any surface fat and return the braising juices to the casserole. Stir in the dissolved potato starch. Then bring the sauce to a boil over high heat, stirring constantly until it is lightly thickened and smooth. Reduce the heat to low, gently stir in the caviar and lemon juice and taste for seasoning. Pour the sauce over the veal and serve at once, or if you prefer, serve the sauce separately.

Täidetud Vasikarind *(Baltic States)*
ROAST STUFFED SHOULDER OF VEAL

To serve 8 to 10

½ pound ground lean veal
½ pound ground lean pork
½ pound ground lean beef
½ cup fresh bread crumbs, made
    from homemade-style white bread,
    pulverized in a blender or finely
    shredded with a fork
1 cup finely chopped onions

2 eggs
Salt
Freshly ground black pepper
A 5-pound boned shoulder of veal
4 hard-cooked eggs, peeled
1½-2 cups cold water, or 1½-2 cups
    chicken stock, fresh or canned
½ cup sour cream

To make the stuffing, combine the ground veal, pork and beef in a large mixing bowl, and add the bread crumbs, onions, water, eggs, 1 tablespoon of salt and 1 teaspoon of pepper. Mix with your hands or a large spoon until all the ingredients are well combined. Then vigorously knead the mixture for 3 to 5 minutes, or until smooth.

Preheat the oven to 350°. Skin-side down, spread the veal shoulder flat on a table and, with a small, sharp knife, make small cuts in the thickest areas of the meat so that it lies even flatter. Lay a sheet of wax paper over the veal and with the side of a cleaver or meat pounder, pound the meat to a fairly uniform thickness. Remove the paper and sprinkle the veal liberally with salt and somewhat more discreetly with pepper.

Spread half the stuffing on the veal, leaving a 2-inch border of the veal exposed all around the sides. Lay the hard-cooked eggs in a row down the length of the stuffing and spread the remaining stuffing in a layer over them. Bring one long side of the veal over the filling to the middle, and tuck in the two ends. Now bring the other side over the filling, enclosing it snugly. With strong kitchen cord, tie the rolled veal crosswise at 2-inch intervals, then with more cord tie it lengthwise.

Place the rolled veal seam-side down in a shallow roasting pan just large enough to hold it comfortably. Pour in 1½ cups of cold water or chicken stock and roast for 2 hours, undisturbed, basting the veal from time to time with the pan juices.

When the meat is a deep golden brown, carefully transfer it to a serving platter and cut off and discard the strings.

Bring the juices remaining in the pan to a boil over high heat. If most of the liquid has cooked away, add the remaining ½ cup of water or chicken stock to the pan, meanwhile scraping into it any brown bits that may be clinging to the bottom and sides of the pan. Off the heat, stir the ½ cup of sour cream into the sauce, a tablespoon at a time. Taste for seasoning and pour into a sauceboat.

Slice the roll crosswise into 1-inch rounds and arrange them slightly overlapping down the center of a large heated platter. Moisten them with a few tablespoons of sauce and serve the remaining sauce separately.

Shashlyk (Caucasus)
GEORGIAN SKEWERED LAMB

To serve 4

1 large onion, peeled and finely grated
1 tablespoon strained fresh lemon
   juice
1 tablespoon olive oil
1 teaspoon salt
¼ teaspoon freshly ground black
   pepper
2 pounds boneless leg or shoulder

of lamb, trimmed of excess fat
   and cut into 1- to 1½-inch cubes
2 medium onions, cut into ¼-inch-
   thick chunks

GARNISH
2 medium firm, ripe tomatoes, cut
   into eighths
10 scallions, trimmed
1 lemon, quartered

In a large mixing bowl, beat together the grated onion, lemon juice, olive oil, salt and pepper. Add the meat and let it marinate for at least 3 hours at room temperature, tossing it about in the marinade every hour or so to keep the pieces well moistened.

Light a layer of coals in a charcoal broiler and burn until a white ash appears on the surface, or preheat your kitchen broiler to its highest point.

String the cubes of lamb tightly on 4 long skewers, alternating the lamb with the chunks of onion; press them firmly together. Broil 4 inches from the source of heat, turning the skewers occasionally, until the lamb is done to your taste and the onions are brown. For pink lamb, allow about 10 minutes; for well-done lamb, more typical of Georgian cooking, allow about 15 minutes. Slide the lamb and onions off the skewers onto heated individual plates, and serve with the raw tomatoes, scallions and lemon quarters.

Hakklihakotlet *(Baltic States)*
ESTONIAN GROUND MEAT PATTIES

To serve 4

½ pound lean ground beef	shredded with a fork
½ pound lean ground veal	1 teaspoon salt
½ pound lean ground pork	¼ teaspoon freshly ground black
2 eggs	pepper
1 cup fresh bread crumbs, made	½ cup finely chopped onions
from homemade-style white bread,	¾ cup cold water
pulverized in a blender or freshly	4 tablespoons vegetable oil

Combine the beef, veal, pork, eggs, ½ cup of the bread crumbs, salt, pepper, onions and water in a large mixing bowl and knead with your hands for 5 or 10 minutes until the mixture is smooth, light and fluffy.

Moisten your hands with cold water and shape the mixture into 8 thick, round patties, then dip them each in the remaining ½ cup of breadcrumbs, coating both sides thoroughly.

Heat the 4 tablespoons of oil in a heavy 10- to 12-inch skillet over high heat until a light haze forms above it. Fry the patties 4 at a time about 5 minutes on each side, regulating the heat so that they brown deeply without burning. To make sure they are fully cooked insert the tip of a small knife into one of the patties, spreading it slightly apart. The meat should show no sign of pink. If it does, lower the heat and cook the patties a few minutes longer. Serve at once, accompanied perhaps by braised red cabbage *(Recipe Index)*.

Liulia-Kebab *(Caucasus)*
GROUND LAMB SAUSAGES

To serve 4

	6 tablespoons finely cut fresh mint
2 pounds lean ground lamb	leaves, or substitute 3 tablespoons
¼ cup finely chopped onions	crumbled dry mint
2 teaspoons salt	8 scallions, trimmed, thoroughly
Freshly ground black pepper	washed and dried

Light a layer of coals in a charcoal broiler and burn until a white ash appears on the surface; or preheat your kitchen broiler to its highest point.

In a large mixing bowl, combine the ground lamb, onions, salt, a few grindings of pepper and the mint. Beat with a large wooden spoon until the mixture is smooth, then divide it into 8 equal parts. Dip your hands into cold water and shape the portions into 3½- to 4-inch-long sausages, about 2 inches thick. Thread the sausages lengthwise onto 4 skewers, leaving about ¼ inch between each sausage.

If you are broiling the sausages in an oven broiler, suspend the skewers side by side across the length of a roasting pan deep enough to allow a 1-inch space below the meat. Broil 4 inches from the source of the heat, turning the skewers from time to time, until the meat is golden brown and done to your taste. For pink lamb, broil about 10 minutes; well-done lamb (Armenians always cook it to this stage) will take 3 or 4 minutes longer. With the side of a knife or fork carefully slide the sausages off the skewers onto heated plates and serve with the scallions.

Karabakh Khorovats (Caucasus)
SKEWERED PORK WITH POMEGRANATE SYRUP

To serve 4

	2 teaspoons salt
1 tablespoon oregano	Freshly ground black pepper
1 large onion, finely grated	2 pounds boneless lean pork, cut
1 tablespoon olive oil	from the loin, cut into 1½- to 2-
2 tablespoons pomegranate syrup	inch cubes

In a large bowl, combine the oregano, grated onions, olive oil, pomegranate syrup, salt and a few grindings of black pepper. Add the pork, stir thoroughly, and marinate at room temperature for 3 to 4 hours, turning the pork about in the marinade every hour or so to keep it well moistened.

Light a layer of coals in a charcoal broiler and burn until a white ash appears on the surface, or preheat your kitchen broiler to its highest point.

GARNISH
2 medium tomatoes, quartered	washed and dried
8 scallions, trimmed, thoroughly	Pomegranate syrup

Remove the pork from its marinade and string the cubes tightly on 4 skewers, pressing them firmly together. Broil 4 inches from the source of the heat for 15 or 20 minutes, turning the skewers frequently so that the pork browns well on all sides. Slide the pork off the skewers onto individual heated plates and garnish each serving with the tomatoes and scallions. Serve the bowl of pomegranate syrup separately.

Golubtsy *(Russian)*

STUFFED CABBAGE ROLLS IN SOUR-CREAM SAUCE

To serve 6

A 3-pound head of white cabbage	15 minutes in cold water and
12 tablespoons butter (1½ quarter-	drained
pound sticks)	2 tablespoons vegetable oil
3 cups finely chopped onions	3 medium tomatoes, peeled, seeded
¼ cup long-grain unconverted rice	and chopped, *(see borshch ukraïnsky,*
¾ pound lean ground beef	*page 21)*
1 teaspoon salt	1 tablespoon flour
Freshly ground black pepper	½ cup sour cream
12 to 16 prunes, pitted and soaked	¼ cup finely cut fresh dill leaves

Drop the cabbage into a large pot of boiling water and let it cook briskly for about 10 minutes. Remove the cabbage (letting the water continue to boil) and carefully detach as many of the outer leaves as you can until it becomes difficult to separate them. Return the cabbage to the boiling water and cook for a few minutes longer. Remove and again detach as many more leaves as you can. Repeat this process until the whole cabbage has been separated into individual leaves. (Discard the smallest inner leaves.)

Bring 2 cups of water to a boil in a 1-quart saucepan, add the rice and boil briskly, uncovered, for about 12 minutes. Drain in a sieve and set aside.

In a heavy 10- to 12-inch skillet, melt 4 tablespoons of the butter over high heat. Add 2 cups of the onions and, stirring occasionally, cook 8 to 10 minutes, or until they are soft and lightly browned. Transfer them to a large mixing bowl and add the ground meat, rice, 1 teaspoon of the salt and a few grindings of pepper. Mix together until well combined and stir in the prunes. Taste for seasoning.

Lay the cabbage leaves side by side and, with a small knife, trim the base of each leaf of its tough rib end. Place ¼ cup of the filling and 1 prune in the center of each of the 12 largest leaves, less filling on the smaller leaves, and roll up all of the leaves tightly, neatly tucking in the ends as if you were wrapping a package.

Preheat the oven to 325°. In a heavy 10- to 12-inch skillet, melt 4 tablespoons of the butter in the 2 tablespoons of oil over high heat. When the foam begins to subside, add 4 or 6 cabbage rolls, seam-sides down, and fry 3 to 5 minutes on each side, or until golden brown. Watch carefully for any sign of burning, and regulate the heat accordingly. With a slotted spoon, transfer the rolls to a shallow ovenproof baking dish just large enough to hold them in one layer and proceed to brown the remaining rolls similarly.

Melt the remaining 4 more tablespoons of butter in the skillet and add the remaining cup of chopped onions. Cook 3 or 4 minutes, or until the onions are soft and translucent, then stir in the chopped tomatoes, the remaining teaspoon of salt and a few grindings of pepper. In a small mixing bowl, beat the flour into the sour cream a teaspoon at a time and stir the mixture into the simmering sauce. Taste for seasoning and pour the sauce over the cabbage rolls, masking them completely. Bake uncovered in the center of the oven for 45 minutes, or until the rolls are golden brown. Sprinkle with chopped dill and serve at once.

Kapsarullid *(Baltic States)*
ESTONIAN STUFFED CABBAGE

To serve 4

1 large white cabbage (4 pounds)
1 tablespoon salt
½ pound ground lean veal
½ pound ground lean pork
½ pound ground lean beef
½ cup finely chopped onions
¾ cup cold water
1 cup fine dry breadcrumbs

2 eggs
¼ teaspoon freshly ground black pepper
2 teaspoons salt
3 tablespoons butter, cut into thin slices
1 cup canned, uncooked lingonberries or cranberries, crushed

Drop the whole cabbage and 1 tablespoon of salt into a 6-quart pot of boiling water and boil briskly, uncovered, for about 10 minutes. Remove the cabbage to a plate (let the water continue to boil) and carefully detach as many of the softened outer leaves as you can. Return the cabbage to the boiling water and cook for a few minutes longer. Remove from the water and again detach the softened leaves, repeating this process until you have separated the whole cabbage into individual leaves. Spread the leaves in one layer on paper towels and pat them dry.

In a large mixing bowl, combine the ground meats, onions, water, breadcrumbs, eggs, pepper and salt and beat with a large spoon until smooth. Place 2 large cabbage leaves side by side, slightly overlapping, and place a third leaf on top of them. Spoon ½ cup of the filling in the center of the leaves, cover with a fourth leaf, and roll up, tucking in the sides as you proceed. Make similar cabbage rolls with the remaining ingredients.

Preheat the oven to 300°. Arrange the stuffed cabbage rolls, seam-side down, in a baking dish just large enough to hold them in one layer. Pour ½ cup cold water into the dish and top each roll with a slice of the butter. Bake in the center of the oven, basting from time to time with the juices in the pan, for 2 to 2½ hours, or until the rolls are golden brown. Serve hot, accompanied by a bowl of crushed lingonberries or cranberries.

Zharennyi Porosenok *(Russia)*

ROAST SUCKLING PIG

Roast suckling pig is a popular main course at Soviet feasts. The smaller the suckling pig the more succulent it usually is. Although usually presented whole, the pig is often more conveniently roasted in quarters as it is here.

To serve 8 to 10

A 10- to 12-pound suckling pig, the head removed and the body cut into quarters

2 tablespoons coarse salt
2 teaspoons freshly ground black pepper
¼ cup vegetable oil

Preheat the oven to 350°. Wash the pig under cold running water and pat it thoroughly dry with paper towels. Sprinkle the flesh liberally with the coarse salt and pepper and rub them into the cavities with your fingers. With a pastry brush, coat the skin and flesh of the quarters and the head of the pig with vegetable oil. Crumple a sheet of aluminum foil into a small ball and insert it into the pig's mouth to keep it open as it roasts. Wrap small sheets of foil around the ears, to prevent them from burning.

Place the head in the center of a rack set in a shallow roasting pan and arrange the quarters skin-side up around it. Roast the pig undisturbed for 1¼ to 1½ hours, or until the skin is crisp and the juices run clear when the pig's flesh is pierced with the tip of a sharp knife. Fifteen minutes or so before the pig is done, remove the foil from the ears to brown them slightly.

Serve the pig on a bed of hot *kasha (Recipe Index),* placing the head in the center with the quarters around it. Replace the foil in the mouth with a fresh apple.

RICE
KASHA

Uzbek Palov *(Central Asia)*

RICE PILAF WITH LAMB AND VEGETABLES

To serve 6

1/4 cup vegetable oil

1 pound boneless shoulder of lamb, cut into 1-inch cubes

3 large carrots, scraped and cut into strips 1/4 inch wide and 2 inches long

2 large onions, peeled and cut into strips about 1/4 inch wide and 2 inches long (about 31/2 cups)

3 cups unconverted, long-grain white rice

2 teaspoons salt

1/2 teaspoon freshly ground black pepper

6 cups cold water

Heat the oil in a heavy 10- to 12-inch skillet over high heat until a light haze forms above it. Drop in the lamb cubes and fry them for 5 to 8 minutes, turning them constantly with a large spoon until they are lightly and evenly browned on all sides. With a slotted spoon transfer the cubes of lamb to a heavy 4-quart casserole.

To the fat remaining in the pan, add the carrots and 3 cups of the onions. Stirring frequently, cook the vegetables over moderate heat until they are soft but not brown, then stir in the rice. Reduce the heat to low and, stirring constantly, cook about 2 minutes, or until the rice becomes somewhat opaque and is thoroughly coated with the oil.

With a rubber spatula, transfer the contents of the pan to the casserole of meat and sprinkle with the salt and pepper. Toss lightly to combine the ingredients, then pour in 6 cups of water and bring to a boil over high heat. Reduce the heat to low, cover the casserole and simmer 20 minutes, or until the rice is tender and has absorbed most of its cooking liquid. Taste for seasoning.

Transfer the pilaf to a serving bowl or platter and scatter the remaining 1/2 cup of raw onions over the top. Serve at once, accompanied if you like by flat onion bread *(Recipe Index)*.

Chrov Plav *(Caucasus)*
RICE PILAF WITH DRIED FRUIT AND NUTS

To serve 4

2 tablespoons currants
4 medium prunes, pitted and cut
 lengthwise into narrow strips
4 tablespoons butter
¼ cup dried apricots, cut into narrow
strips
¼ cup finely chopped blanched
 untoasted almonds
1 tablespoon honey
1 cup long-grain unconverted white
 rice

Soak the currants and prunes in a bowl of warm water for 15 minutes, then drain and pat them dry with paper towels.

Melt the butter in a 10- to 12-inch skillet or casserole over high heat and add the apricots, currants, prunes and almonds. Reduce the heat to low and cook uncovered for 3 to 5 minutes, or until the nuts are lightly colored. Stir in the honey and rice, cover with 2 cups of water and bring to a boil over high heat. Reduce the heat to low, cover the pan and simmer 25 minutes, or until the liquid has been absorbed. Serve hot, as a main course for lunch or an accompaniment to *karabakh khorovats* *(Recipe Index)*.

Azerbaijan Pilaf *(Caucasus)*
RICE WITH ALMONDS AND SESAME SEEDS

To serve 4 to 6

½ cup sliced blanched almonds
2 tablespoons butter
1 cup unconverted long-grain rice
2 cups chicken stock, fresh or canned
½ teaspoon white sesame seeds
¼ teaspoon ground ginger
¼ teaspoon salt
Freshly ground black pepper

Preheat the oven to 350°. Spread the almonds on a cookie sheet in a single layer and toast in the oven for about 5 minutes, watching for any sign of burning and regulate the heat accordingly. Set aside.

Melt the butter in a heavy 1½- to 2-quart casserole set over moderate heat. Add the rice and stir with a wooden spoon until the rice turns somewhat white and opaque. Stir in the sesame seeds, then pour in the chicken stock, ginger, salt and a few grindings of black pepper. Stirring constantly, bring to a boil, then cover the casserole tightly and bake in the center of the oven for 20 to 25 minutes, or until the liquid has all been absorbed and the rice is tender. Sprinkle the reserved almonds over the rice and serve at once.

Kasha *(Russia)*

BUCKWHEAT GROATS WITH MUSHROOMS AND ONIONS

To serve 6

1 cup coarse *kasha* (buckwheat groats)	butter
1 egg	2 to 3 cups boiling water
1 teaspoon salt	2 cups finely chopped onions
8 tablespoons (¼-pound stick)	½ pound fresh mushrooms, finely chopped

In a mixing bowl, toss the *kasha* and egg together with a large wooden spoon until the grains are thoroughly coated. Transfer to an ungreased, 10- to 12-inch skillet (preferably one with a nonstick surface) and cook uncovered over moderate heat, stirring constantly, until the *kasha* is lightly toasted and dry. Watch carefully for any sign of burning and regulate the heat accordingly. Add the salt, 3 tablespoons of the butter and 2 cups of boiling water. Stir thoroughly, cover the pan tightly, and reduce the heat to low. Simmer, stirring occasionally, for about 20 minutes. If at this point the *kasha* is not yet tender and seems dry, stir in the additional cup of boiling water and cook covered 10 minutes longer, or until the water is absorbed and the grains of *kasha* are separate and fluffy. Remove the pan from the heat, remove the cover, and let the *kasha* rest undisturbed for about 10 minutes.

Meanwhile, melt 3 tablespoons of the butter in a heavy 10- to 12-inch skillet over high heat. Add the chopped onions, lower the heat to moderate, and, stirring frequently, fry for 3 or 4 minutes, or until the onions are soft and pale gold. Stir the onions into the *kasha* and melt the remaining 2 tablespoons of butter in the skillet over high heat. Drop in the mushrooms, reduce the heat to moderate, and cook 2 or 3 minutes, stirring frequently. Then raise the heat to high and cook the mushrooms briskly, uncovered, until all the liquid in the pan has evaporated. Add the mushrooms to the *kasha* and onions and toss together. Taste for seasoning.

Kasha may be cooked in advance and reheated, covered, in a preheated 200° oven for 20 minutes or so. Or, it may be steamed by placing the cooked *kasha* in a colander and setting the colander over a deep pot filled with 1 inch of water. Drape the colander with a towel, bring the water to a boil and steam the *kasha* for about 10 minutes, or until it is heated through.

BREADS
DUMPLINGS

Non (*Central Asia*)
FLAT ONION BREADS

To make 16 breads

6 tablespoons butter	115°)
1½ cups finely chopped onions	1 teaspoon salt
¾ cup lukewarm water (110° to	2½ to 3 cups all-purpose flour

Melt 1 tablespoon of the butter in a heavy 10- to 12-inch skillet set over high heat. Add the onions, reduce the heat to low and, stirring occasionally, cook 3 to 5 minutes, or until the onions are soft but not brown. Transfer them to a bowl and cool to room temperature.

Melt the remaining butter in the skillet and pour it into a large mixing bowl. Add the lukewarm water and, with a large spoon, stir in the chopped onions, salt and 2½ cups of the flour, ½ cup at a time. If necessary, beat in as much of the remaining ½ cup of flour as you need to make a dough that does not stick to your fingers. Gather the dough into a large, compact ball and divide it into 16 pieces. With the palms of your hands, shape each piece of dough into a 1½- to 2-inch ball. Then, with a lightly floured rolling pin, roll out the balls one at a time into circles that are about 8 inches in diameter. Set the rounds of dough aside.

Set a heavy 10- to 12-inch ungreased pan over high heat. When it is hot enough for a drop of water flicked across its surface to instantly evaporate, place 1 round of dough in the center. Brown for 3 or 4 minutes on each side, turning it over with your fingers or a wide spatula; do not be concerned if the bread does not brown evenly.

Transfer the bread to a rack to dry and proceed to fry and dry the remaining dough similarly. Serve the bread in a basket or other porous container. If for any reason the bread becomes limp after a day or so, place the rounds in a single layer on a cookie sheet and bake them for 5 to 10 minutes in a preheated 250° oven until they freshen.

Lašinēčiai *(Baltic States)*
BACON BUNS

To make about 3 dozen buns

1 package active dry yeast	10 tablespoons unsalted butter,
1 cup lukewarm milk (110° to 115°)	softened
2 tablespoons sugar	1 pound lean bacon, finely shredded
1 teaspoon salt	1 cup finely chopped onions
3 cups all-purpose flour	1 egg yolk mixed with 1 tablespoon
3 egg yolks	cream

Sprinkle the yeast into ½ cup of the lukewarm milk. Add the sugar and salt and stir until thoroughly dissolved. Place the mixture in a warm, draft-free place, such as an unlighted oven, for 5 to 8 minutes, or until the mixture has begun to bubble and almost doubled in volume.

Pour the flour into a large mixing bowl and make a deep well in the center. Drop in the yeast mixture, egg yolks, the remaining ½ cup of milk and 8 tablespoons of the butter and, with a large wooden spoon, slowly stir the flour into the liquid ingredients. Beat vigorously until a fairly firm dough is formed. Cover the bowl loosely with a kitchen towel and place it in the warm draft-free spot for 45 minutes to an hour, or until the dough has doubled in bulk. Then punch the dough down with your fist, cover loosely, and let it rise another 45 minutes, or until it again doubles in bulk.

Meanwhile, prepare the filling. Stirring occasionally, fry the bacon and chopped onions in a large skillet over moderate heat. When the bacon has rendered all its fat and the onions are tender and lightly colored, drain them through a fine sieve. Discard the fat and set the bacon and onions aside.

With a pastry brush, lightly coat 2 cookie sheets with a tablespoon of butter each. Cut the dough in half and, on a lightly floured surface, roll each half into a circle about ⅛ inch thick. With a 2 ½- to 3-inch cookie cutter, cut out about 18 rounds of dough. Drop 1 teaspoon of the bacon mixture in the center of each and fold in the sides of the circle, making a neat packet. Set the buns, seam-side down, on the cookie sheet, leaving 1 inch between them. Roll and fill the remaining dough similarly. Place the cookie sheets in the warm, draft-free spot for 15 to 20 minutes, or until the buns almost double in size.

Preheat the oven to 375°. Bake the buns in the center of the oven for 10 minutes, then, with a pastry brush, coat each bun with the egg yolk-and-cream mixture. Bake another 10 minutes, or until golden brown. Serve the buns hot; if you cool them after baking, reheat for 10 minutes or so in a 325° oven.

"Khachapuri": A high-rising Georgian Cheese Bread for Hearty Diners

Fold a 22-inch circle of dough into quarters and place the point of the wedge at the center of a 9-inch tin.

Unfold the dough, draping the outer rim of the circle over the edge of the pan. Smooth out the center.

After mounding the cheese filling high in the center begin to fold in excess dough hanging over the tin.

Draw the sides of the dough up over the filling into the center, pleating the dough into loose folds.

Rotate the tin as you continue to pleat the dough. Try to make the pleats even all around the tin.

Gather together the ends of the dough that meet in the center and twist them into a small knob.

Place 2 tablespoons of the cheese filling on a 4½-inch circle of dough and form the cheese into a diamond.	With your fingers, roll the edges of the dough up over the edge of the filling, following the diamond shape.	Perfect the final shape of the tartlet by pinching each of the four corners of the diamond to a sharp point.

Khachapuri (*Caucasus*)
GEORGIAN CHEESE BREAD

Georgian cheese bread is made either as individual open tarts or large round or oblong loaves. (The small tarts are so popular in the Caucasus that they are sold by street vendors.) Both the loaves and the tarts are well-suited to brunch or breakfast, and the tarts might make an unusual accompaniment to cocktails or tea.

To make 48 cheese tarts or 1 large
   loaf

DOUGH	3½ to 4 cups all-purpose flour
2 packages active dry yeast	2 teaspoons salt
½ teaspoon plus 1 tablespoon sugar	8 tablespoons butter, softened (¼-
1 cup lukewarm milk (110° to 115°)	pound stick)

Sprinkle the 2 packages of yeast and the ½ teaspoon of the sugar over ½ cup of the lukewarm milk in a small, shallow bowl. Set aside for 2 or 3 minutes, then stir until the yeast is thoroughly dissolved. Place in a warm, draft-free spot (such as an unlighted oven) for 5 to 8 minutes, or until the mixture has doubled in volume.

    Pour 3 cups of the flour into a large mixing bowl and make a deep well in the center. Add the remaining ½ cup of milk, the yeast mixture, the remaining 1 tablespoon of sugar, 2 teaspoons of salt and 8 tablespoons of butter. With a large spoon, slowly beat the flour into these ingredients and

Continued on next page
73

continue to beat vigorously until smooth. Gather the dough into a ball and place it on a lightly floured surface.

Knead the dough by folding it end to end, then pressing it down, pushing it forward with the heel of your hand and folding it back. Knead in this fashion for at least 10 minutes, sprinkling the dough every few minutes with small handfuls of as much of the remaining flour as you need to prevent it from sticking to the board.

When the dough is smooth and elastic, place it in a large, lightly buttered bowl. Dust the dough lightly with flour and cover the bowl loosely with a kitchen towel. Let the dough rise in the warm, draft-free place for about 45 minutes to an hour, or until it has doubled in bulk and springs back slowly when gently poked with a finger. Then punch the dough down with a blow of your fist and set aside again to rise for another 30 to 40 minutes or until it again doubles in bulk.

FILLING
2 pounds sweet Muenster cheese,
    finely grated by hand or in
    a blender
2 tablespoons butter, softened

1 egg
1 egg, lightly beaten (for tarts)
2 tablespoons finely chopped
    coriander *(cilantro)* (optional, for
    the tarts)

Meanwhile, prepare the cheese filling. In a large mixing bowl, combine the grated cheese, softened butter and the whole egg. Beat vigorously with a large spoon until smooth, then purée in a food mill or rub it with the back of a spoon through a fine sieve set over a large bowl.

Preheat the oven to 375°. To make the round loaf, punch the dough down with a sharp blow of your fist, then roll it on a lightly floured surface into a circle about 22 inches in diameter.

Following the illustrations on page 72, use the dough to line a buttered layer-cake tin 9 inches round by 1½ inches deep. Then fill it with the cheese mixture, and fold in the ends of dough. Set the loaf aside to rest for 10 or 15 minutes, then bake the bread in the center of the oven for 1 hour, or until golden brown. Turn the bread out onto a wire cake rack and cool a little before serving.

To make individual tarts, roll the dough into a 24-inch-wide circle and with a 4½-inch cookie cutter, cut out 48 rounds. Following the illustrations on page 73, fill and shape the rounds. Set them side by side on buttered cookie sheets and brush the dough with lightly beaten egg. Let the tarts rest for 10 minutes, then bake them in the center of the oven for 20 to 25 minutes, or until golden brown. With a wide spatula, transfer the tarts to a serving platter, sprinkle with chopped coriander, if you like, and serve warm.

Churek *(Caucasus)*

FLAT ARMENIAN BREAD WITH SESAME SEEDS

To make 10 large rounds

1 package dry active yeast	6 cups all-purpose flour
1 tablespoon sugar	¼ pound unsalted butter, melted
2¼ cups lukewarm water (110° to 115°)	1 tablespoon salt
	2 tablespoons white sesame seeds

Sprinkle the yeast and 1 teaspoon of the sugar into ¼ cup of the lukewarm water in a small, shallow bowl. Let it stand 2 or 3 minutes, then stir to dissolve the yeast completely. Set the bowl aside in a warm, draft-free spot (such as an unlighted oven) for about 5 to 10 minutes, or until the mixture almost doubles in volume.

Pour the flour into a large mixing bowl and make a well in the center. Pour in the yeast mixture, remaining water, melted butter, remaining sugar and salt. With a large spoon, beat the flour into the liquid ingredients, continuing to beat for as long as 10 minutes, or until a soft, spongy dough is formed. Cover loosely with a kitchen towel and set aside in the warm, draft-free spot until the mixture doubles in volume.

Preheat the oven to 350°. Place the dough on a lightly floured surface and divide it into 10 equal parts. Roll out each part as thinly as possible into circles, then place 2 or 3 circles on a cookie sheet. Sprinkle lightly with cold water and a few sesame seeds and set the cookie sheet on the floor of the oven. Bake about 20 minutes, or until the bread is a pale golden brown. Transfer the breads with a wide spatula to a wire cake rack and bake the remaining rounds similarly. The bread will keep several days at room temperature if wrapped securely in foil.

Pelmeni (*Russia*)
SIBERIAN MEAT DUMPLINGS

Although 6 dozen meat dumplings may seem a large quantity to make at one time, Russians, who are traditionally hearty eaters, expect to be served at least a dozen apiece. As they have done for centuries, Siberians still make large quantities of "pelmeni" and freeze them uncooked in the deep snow surrounding their homes. A modern freezer will do the job even better. Simply defrost the "pelmeni" and boil them in any quantity you desire.

To make about 6 dozen

DOUGH
1 teaspoon salt

3 eggs
1 cup water
4 to 4½ cups all-purpose flour

DOUGH: In a large mixing bowl, combine the flour and salt and make a deep well in the center. Drop in the eggs and water and, with your hands or a large spoon, slowly but thoroughly mix the flour into the liquid ingredients until the mixture can be gathered into a compact ball. Transfer the dough to a lightly floured surface and knead it by folding it end to end, then pressing it down and pushing it forward several times with the heel of your hand. Sprinkle the dough with extra flour when necessary to prevent it from sticking to the board. Knead for about 10 minutes, or until the dough is smooth and elastic. Then shape it into a ball, wrap it loosely in wax paper, and let it rest at room temperature for at least 1 hour.

FILLING
2 tablespoons butter
1 tablespoon vegetable oil
½ cup finely chopped onions
6 ounces lean top round or beef

chuck, ground twice
6 ounces fresh pork fat, ground twice
1 teaspoon salt
½ teaspoon freshly ground black
  pepper

FILLING: In a heavy 10- to 12-inch skillet, melt the butter in the oil over high heat. When the foam has almost subsided, add the chopped onions and, stirring frequently, cook over moderate heat for 3 or 4 minutes, or until they are soft and lightly colored. With a rubber spatula scrape the onions into a large mixing bowl. Then add the meat, pork fat, salt, pepper and ½ cup of cold water and mix with a large spoon or your hands until the ingredients are well combined and the mixture is smooth.

On a lightly floured surface, roll the reserved dough into a rough rectangle about ⅛ inch thick. Lift the dough over the back of your hands and pull your hands apart, stretching the dough carefully until it is almost paper thin. Spread it on a table and, with a sharp knife, trim it into an 18-inch square. Cut out rounds of the dough with a 2½- to 3-inch cookie cutter.

Drop ¾ teaspoon of the filling in the lower half of each round, run a finger lightly dipped in water around the edges and fold the exposed dough over the filling. Seal the edges by pressing firmly with the prongs of a fork. Dip your fingers in water again and lift up the two corners, pinching them together to form a triangular pouch.

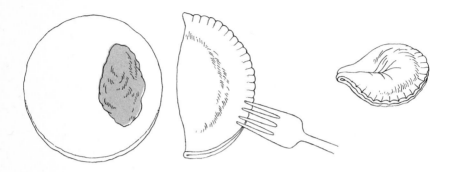

Over high heat bring 3 quarts of water to a vigorous boil in a 4- to 6-quart casserole. Drop about a dozen of the dumplings into the water, reduce the heat to low, and cook them uncovered for 8 to 10 minutes, or until they rise to the surface of the water. With a slotted spoon, transfer them to a double thickness of paper towels and let them drain while you cook and drain the remaining dumplings similarly.

½ cup melted butter or 1 cup sour cream (optional)

The *pelmeni* may be served in either of two ways: As individual portions with melted butter or sour cream, or as a garnish for a clear soup such as beef or chicken broth.

Manty *(Central Asia)*
UZBEK LAMB DUMPLINGS

To serve 6

FILLING
1½ pounds lean lamb, finely ground
1½ cups finely chopped onions

2 teaspoons salt
½ teaspoon freshly ground black
  pepper
7 tablespoons butter

For the filling, mix the ground lamb, chopped onions, salt and pepper in a mixing bowl and beat with a wooden spoon until well combined.

DOUGH
3 cups flour

1½ cups water

Pour the flour into a large mixing bowl, make a deep well in the center and pour in the water. Mix vigorously until smooth, then gather the dough into a ball and transfer it to a lightly floured surface. Roll out into a rectangle about ¹⁄₁₆ inch thick. With a 4½-inch cookie cutter, cut out 18 to 20 circles of dough and spoon about 5 teaspoons of filling in the center of each.

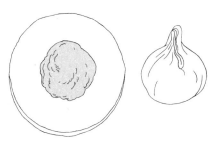

Top each circle with 1 teaspoon of the butter and draw up the sides of the circle so that they meet in the middle, enclosing the filling. Dip your fingers in water, pinch the top closed and twist it to form a small pouch.

¼ cup finely cut fresh dill leaves or
  fresh mint

¾ cup unflavored yoghurt

Steam the *manty* in the following fashion: Pour enough water into a large kettle to come about 1 inch up the side. Bring to a boil over moderate heat and set a colander into the kettle. Place the *manty* in the colander, cover the kettle securely and lower the heat. Steam for 15 minutes, then transfer the *manty* to individual bowls or to a large serving bowl. Sprinkle with the dill or mint and serve with yoghurt, either as an accompaniment to soup or alone as a light luncheon dish.

Chebureki *(Central Asia)*
DEEP-FRIED LAMB DUMPLINGS

These fried lamb dumplings are a Tatar dish, developed in the Crimea and brought to Central Asia, where many Tatars now live.

To make 38 dumplings

3 tablespoons butter
1 tablespoon vegetable oil
¾ pound lean lamb, finely ground twice
¼ cup finely chopped parsley
2 tablespoons finely chopped fresh
coriander *(cilantro)*
2 teaspoons salt
3 tablespoons cold boiled white rice
1 recipe *pelmeni* dough *(page 76)*
1 egg, lightly beaten
Vegetable oil for deep-frying

Melt the 3 tablespoons of butter in 1 tablespoon of vegetable oil in a heavy 10- to 12-inch skillet set over high heat. When the fat just begins to brown lightly, add the ground lamb. Mashing the meat constantly with a fork to break up any lumps, cook for 3 to 5 minutes, or until the lamb is light brown. Transfer to a large mixing bowl and with a large spoon or your hands, toss with the chopped parsley, coriander, salt and rice. Cool to room temperature.

On a lightly floured surface, roll the dough until it is about ⅛ inch thick. Lift the dough over the backs of your hands and spread your hands apart gently until the dough stretches almost paper thin. Lay it flat on the table and with a 2½- to 3-inch cookie cutter, cut out 76 rounds of the dough. Top half of the rounds with a heaping teaspoon of filling and flatten the filling slightly. Cover with the remaining rounds and seal the edges by pressing them firmly all around their circumference with the prongs of a fork. With a pastry brush, coat the edges of the dumplings with the beaten egg to seal them even more securely.

Heat the oil in a deep-fat fryer until it reaches a temperature of 375° on a deep-frying thermometer. Fry the dumplings, 6 to 8 at a time, for 2 or 3 minutes, turning them over in the fat until they are evenly browned. Drain on paper towels and serve hot, with soup or as a first course.

Varenyky z Kvashenoiu Kapustoiu (Ukraine)
SAVORY SAUERKRAUT DUMPLINGS

To make 16 dumplings

4 tablespoons butter
1 pound sauerkraut, washed under
   cold running water, squeezed dry
   and finely chopped
1 cup finely chopped onions
¼ teaspoon sugar

½ teaspoon salt
Freshly ground black pepper
2 tablespoons sour cream
1 recipe *varenyky* dough (*opposite*)
¼ cup melted butter, hot
1 cup sour cream

Melt 1 tablespoon of butter in a heavy 10- to 12-inch enameled or stainless-steel skillet and add the sauerkraut. Fry over low heat, stirring occasionally with a fork, for 3 to 5 minutes, or until the sauerkraut is almost completely dry and has begun to stick lightly to the pan. Then scrape it into a bowl.

   Melt 3 tablespoons of butter in the skillet and add the onions. Stirring occasionally, fry over moderate heat for 5 to 8 minutes, or until the onions are soft but not brown. Return the sauerkraut to the pan, stir in the sugar, salt and a few grindings of pepper and cover tightly. Cook over low heat for 10 to 15 minutes, then, off the heat, stir in the 2 tablespoons of sour cream. Taste for seasoning.

   Following the instructions in the *varenyky* recipe on page 82, roll out the dough and cut it into 3½- to 4-inch circles. Fill each circle with 1 tablespoon of the sauerkraut mixture and fold up and cook as directed. To serve, arrange the dumplings side by side on a heated platter and pour the melted butter over them. Serve with a bowl of sour cream.

Halushky (Ukraine)
FLUFFY EGG DUMPLINGS

To make about 15 dumplings

¾ cup all-purpose flour
¾ cup uncooked farina
2 teaspoons baking powder
3 teaspoons butter, cut into tiny
   bits and chilled

2 eggs, well beaten
¼ cup milk
2 quarts water
Salt
1 cup fried onions (optional)
1 cup sour cream (optional)

In a large, chilled mixing bowl, combine the flour, farina, baking powder and butter. Working quickly, use your fingertips to rub the dry ingredients and butter together until they blend and look like flakes of coarse meal. Drop in the eggs and milk and stir vigorously with a large spoon until the batter is thick and smooth.

Bring 2 quarts of lightly salted water to a boil in a heavy 2½- to 3-quart casserole, then reduce the heat so that the water simmers gently. Dip a tablespoon in cold water, scoop up a tablespoon of batter, and drop it into the simmering water. Repeat—dipping the spoon beforehand in water each time—until 6 tablespoons of the batter have been used. Cover the pan and simmer 6 to 8 minutes until the dumplings have puffed up and have risen to the surface of the water. Remove with a slotted spoon and drain on paper towels while you cook the remaining dumplings. Serve either with a stew or roasted meat, or as a separate course topped with fried onions and sour cream.

Varenyky *(Ukraine)*
DESSERT DUMPLINGS FILLED WITH CHEESE OR FRUIT

To make about 16 dumplings

DOUGH

2 cups all-purpose flour	½ cup milk
1 egg	1 teaspoon salt

DOUGH: Pour the flour into a large mixing bowl and make a deep well in the center. Drop in the egg, milk and salt. With your fingertips or a large spoon, slowly mix the flour into the liquid ingredients, then mix vigorously until the dough is stiff enough to be gathered into a compact ball. If the dough crumbles add an additional 1 to 2 teaspoons of milk to make the particles adhere. Dust the ball with flour, wrap in wax paper, and chill 30 minutes.

CHEESE FILLING

1 pound large-curd cottage or pot cheese	1 tablespoon melted butter, cooled
	½ teaspoon salt
2 tablespoons sugar	2 cups sour cream
1 egg yolk	4 tablespoons melted butter, hot

CHEESE FILLING: Purée the cheese in a food mill, or rub it with the back of a large spoon through a fine sieve set over a bowl. Then beat in the sugar, egg yolk, melted butter and salt, and stir in 1 cup of the sour cream, ¼ cup at a time. Continue to stir until the ingredients are thoroughly mixed. Taste for seasoning; if you prefer the filling sweeter, stir in additional sugar.

Continued on next page

CHERRY FILLING

1½ pounds fresh sour cherries,
   pitted, or substitute 1½ cups
   drained, canned pitted sour
   cherries
⅓ cup sugar

BLUEBERRY FILLING

1 pint blueberries
4 tablespoons sugar
1 tablespoon fresh, strained lemon
   juice
2 egg whites, beaten to a froth

CHERRY OR BLUEBERRY FILLING: Spread half the fruit in the bottom of a 1-quart enameled or stainless-steel saucepan. Sprinkle with half the sugar, then make similar layers of the remaining fruit and sugar. Bring to a boil over high heat, then cover the pan and reduce the heat to low. Simmer over moderate heat for 3 to 5 minutes.

If you are using blueberries, stir in the lemon juice and let them cool to room temperature. With a slotted spoon, transfer the blueberries or sour cherries to a small bowl. Bring the juices remaining in the pan to a rapid boil and boil steadily, uncovered, for 2 or 3 minutes, or until they thicken into a light syrup. Pour the syrup into a small serving bowl and set it aside.

On a lightly floured surface, roll the dough into a circle about ⅛ inch thick. Cut out as many circles as possible with a 3½- to 4-inch cookie cutter. Then gather the remaining scraps into a ball, roll out again, and cut out additional circles. With a pastry brush, coat each circle with a light film of the beaten egg white. Drop 1 tablespoon of the cheese or 1 teaspoon of fruit on the lower half of each circle. Bring the exposed half of the circle up over the filling and press the edges all around the dough firmly with the back of a fork. Make certain that the edges are thoroughly sealed to prevent the filling from seeping through. Set aside, loosely covered with a towel, until ready to cook.

Bring 4 quarts of salted water to a boil in a 5- to 6-quart pot and drop in 6 dumplings. Lower the heat and simmer the dumplings uncovered for 8 to 10 minutes, or until they float to the surface of the water. Remove with a slotted spoon and transfer to a heated platter. Cover loosely with foil to keep them hot while you cook the remaining dumplings similarly.

To serve, arrange the dumplings on a heated platter and moisten them with the hot melted butter. If you have used the fruit filling, serve the dumplings with cherry or blueberry juice. The cheese-filled dumplings are customarily served with the remaining cup of sour cream.

CANDIES DESSERTS

Plombir Slivochnyi *(Russia)*

ICE CREAM

To serve 8 to 10

1½ cups finely chopped glazed
mixed fruits
2 teaspoons vanilla extract
1 teaspoon almond extract

3 cups chilled heavy cream
½ cup confectioners' sugar
½ cup blanched, toasted almonds,
pulverized in a mortar and pestle
or in a nut grinder

In a small mixing bowl, sprinkle the glazed fruits with the vanilla and almond extracts and let them soak for at least 15 minutes.

In a large, chilled mixing bowl, beat the heavy cream with a whisk or rotary or electric beater until it begins to thicken. Gradually beat in the sugar, a tablespoon at a time and continue to beat until the cream holds fairly firm peaks on the beater when it is lifted out of the bowl. With a rubber spatula, fold in the glazed-fruit mixture and the ground almonds and continue to fold until the ingredients are well combined. Transfer the mixture to a 1½-quart soufflé dish or charlotte mold, smooth the top and cover with plastic wrap or foil. Freeze for at least 4 hours, or until firm. To unmold, run a narrow knife or spatula around the inside edge of the ice cream. Then dip the bottom of the mold into hot water for about 15 seconds. Wipe the mold dry, invert a flat serving plate on top of it, and grasping mold and plate firmly together, turn them over. The ice cream should slide out easily. To serve, cut into pie-shaped wedges with a knife dipped in hot water.

Charlottka *(Russia)*

CHARLOTTE RUSSE: LADYFINGERS MOLD WITH CREAM FILLING

To serve 6

12 to 16 ladyfingers, split in half lengthwise	A 2-inch piece of vanilla bean
4 large egg yolks	2 level teaspoons unflavored gelatin, softened in ¼ cup cold water
½ cup sugar	½ cup chilled sour cream
1 cup milk	½ cup chilled heavy cream

Trim 12 of the ladyfinger halves, tapering them slightly at one end. Arrange these halves, side by side, curved sides down, on the bottom of a 1-quart charlotte mold with the tapered ends meeting in the center. Stand the remaining ladyfingers, curved side out, side by side around the inside of the mold; if possible, avoid leaving any open spaces between them.

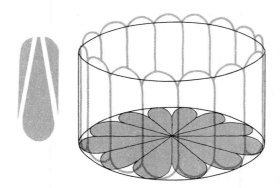

Beat the egg yolks briefly in a mixing bowl with a whisk or an electric or rotary mixer. Still beating, gradually add the sugar, and continue to beat until the mixture is thick and pale yellow and runs sluggishly off the beater when lifted from the bowl. In a small saucepan, warm the milk and vanilla bean over moderate heat until bubbles appear around the edges of the pan. Remove the bean and slowly pour the hot milk into the eggs, beating constantly. Cook over low heat, stirring constantly, until the mixture thickens into a custard heavy enough to coat a spoon. Do not let it boil or it will curdle.

Off the heat, stir in the softened gelatin. When it has completely dissolved, strain the custard through a fine sieve set over a large bowl. With a whisk or rotary or electric beater, whip together the sour cream and heavy cream until the mixture forms stiff peaks on the beater when it is lifted out of the bowl. Fill half a large pot with ice cubes and cover them with 2 inches of water, set the bowl of custard into the pot and stir the custard with a metal spoon for at least 5 minutes, or until it is quite cold and just beginning to thicken to a syrupy consistency. With a rubber spatula, gently fold the whipped cream into the custard. (If by some mischance the cream-and-custard mixture is lumpy, beat it with a whisk until smooth.) Pour the mixture into the prepared mold, smooth the top with a spatula, cover with plastic wrap and refrigerate for 4 or 5 hours.

RASPBERRY PURÉE

2 ten-ounce packages frozen raspberries, defrosted and thoroughly drained

2 tablespoons superfine sugar
1 tablespoon kirsch or any other type of cherry-flavored brandy.

RASPBERRY PURÉE: Rub the raspberries with the back of a large spoon through a fine sieve set over a mixing bowl. Stir in the sugar and kirsch, cover tightly with plastic wrap, and refrigerate until ready to serve.

To unmold the charlotte russe, invert a flat serving plate on top of the mold and, grasping the plate and mold firmly together, turn them over. Gently remove the mold and serve the dessert with a bowl of the raspberry purée.

Babka Yablochnaya (Russia)
APPLE CHARLOTTE WITH APRICOT SAUCE

To serve 8

1 tablespoon unsalted butter, softened
½ pound plus 3 tablespoons unsalted butter, clarified (see tabaka, page 55)
16 slices (½ inch thick) homemade-

style white bread, trimmed of all crusts
5 pounds tart red apples, peeled, cored and thinly sliced (5 quarts)
1 cup sugar
⅓ cup water
1 teaspoon cinnamon

With a pastry brush, lightly coat the bottom and sides of a 1½-quart, 3- to 3½-inch-deep charlotte or other straight-sided mold with the tablespoon of softened butter.

Pour all but 3 tablespoons of the clarified butter into a large bowl. With a sharp knife, cut 3 slices of the bread into 6 triangles by slicing them in half diagonally. Cut another 7 slices of the bread in half. One at a time, briefly dip the bread triangles into the bowl of clarified butter and lay them side by side in the bottom of the mold. With a small, sharp knife, trim the triangles so that their points meet in the middle and no spaces show between the slices. Now dip the bread halves in the butter and stand them upright around the

Continued on next page

sides of the mold, overlapping them slightly. The bread will rise slightly above the top of the mold.

Cut another 3 slices of the bread into 1-inch squares. Heat the 3 reserved tablespoons of clarified butter in a heavy 10- to 12-inch skillet set over high heat and drop in the bread squares. Turning them about constantly with a wooden spoon, cook the squares for 2 to 3 minutes, until they are lightly and evenly colored on all sides. Remove the browned bread squares from the pan with a slotted spoon and set aside.

In a 4-quart casserole combine the apples, sugar and water. Bring to a boil over high heat, then cover tightly, reduce the heat to low, and simmer 30 minutes, or until the apples are tender and show no resistance when pierced with the tip of a sharp knife. Uncover and cook over high heat, stirring frequently, for about 15 minutes, or until most of the liquid has evaporated and the apples become a thick, coarse purée. Stir in the cinnamon and refrigerate the purée until well chilled.

When ready to assemble and bake the dessert, stir the browned bread squares into the thick apple purée and pour the mixture into the prepared mold. Do not be concerned if the filling rises above the rim of the mold; the apple purée will subside as it bakes.

Preheat the oven to 375°. Cut 2 of the remaining slices of bread in half, dip them in the butter and place them on top of the filling. Cut the remaining slice into narrow strips, dip them into the butter and arrange them around the top to cover the exposed areas.

Bake in the center of the oven for 1 hour, or until the bread is golden brown. Cool for 30 minutes at room temperature, then invert a flat serving platter on top and, grasping the plate and mold firmly together, turn them over. Let the mold rest in this fashion for another 30 minutes before gently lifting it off the cake.

APRICOT SAUCE

| 1½ cups apricot preserves (12 ounces) | 2 tablespoons cold water |
| | ¼ cup applejack or Calvados |

APRICOT SAUCE: With the back of a large spoon rub the apricot preserves through a fine sieve set over a 1-quart saucepan. Add the water and cook over moderate heat for about 10 minutes, stirring constantly until the sauce is thick enough to run sluggishly off a spoon when it is lifted from the pan. Off the heat stir in the applejack or Calvados.

Either pour the sauce over the top and sides of the unmolded apple charlotte, or serve it separately in a bowl.

Kisel (*Russia*)
PURÉED FRUIT DESSERT

To make 6 servings of each type

APPLE KISEL

2 pounds tart red apples, peeled,
  cored and cut into 1-inch-thick
  slices (4 cups)
3 cups cold water
½ cup sugar
1 tablespoon potato starch dissolved
  in 1 tablespoon cold water

APRICOT KISEL

½ pound dried apricots (1½ cups)
4½ cups water
4 tablespoons sugar
1 tablespoon potato starch dissolved
  in 1 tablespoon cold water

STRAWBERRY KISEL

2½ pints fresh strawberries, with
  hulls removed
2 cups cold water

¾ cup sugar
1 tablespoon potato starch dissolved
  in 1 tablespoon cold water

CRANBERRY KISEL

3 cups uncooked whole cranberries
  (1½ pints)
2 cups cold water
¾ cup sugar
1 tablespoon potato starch dissolved
  in 1 tablespoon cold water

RHUBARB KISEL

1½ pounds rhubarb, cut into 2-inch
  lengths (4½ cups)
3 cups cold water
¾ cup sugar
1 tablespoon potato starch dissolved
  in 1 tablespoon cold water

Place the apples (or the apricots, strawberries, cranberries or rhubarb) in a 2- to 3-quart enameled or stainless-steel saucepan and pour in the appropriate amount of cold water. Bring to a boil over high heat, then reduce the heat to low and simmer the fruit uncovered for about 10 to 15 minutes, or until the fruit is tender.

With the back of a spoon, rub the fruit mixture through a fine sieve set over a mixing bowl and stir in the appropriate amount of sugar. Return the purée to the pan and bring it to a boil over high heat. Then reduce the heat to moderate, stir in the dissolved potato starch, and, stirring constantly, cook another 2 or 3 minutes, or until the purée just reaches the boil and thickens slightly. Remove from the heat and cool to lukewarm, then pour into individual dessert dishes. Refrigerate for at least 4 hours before serving.

Samsa (*Central Asia*)
SWEET WALNUT FRITTERS

To serve 8 to 10

FILLING
6 ounces walnuts, pulverized in a
    blender or ground in a nut grinder

1½ tablespoons unsalted butter,
    softened
1½ tablespoons sugar

In a large mixing bowl, toss together the walnuts, 1½ tablespoons of butter and the sugar. Set aside at room temperature.

DOUGH
1½ cups all-purpose flour
⅔ cup lukewarm water (110° to 115°)

½ teaspoon salt
4 tablespoons unsalted butter,
    softened

Place the flour in a deep mixing bowl and make a well in the center. Pour in the water, salt and 2 tablespoons of the butter and slowly stir the flour into the other ingredients until well absorbed. Then beat vigorously with a large spoon until a firm dough is formed. Gather the dough into a ball. On a lightly floured surface, roll it into a rectangle approximately 16 inches wide by 18 inches long. Brush the dough with the additional 2 tablespoons of butter and fold it into quarters. Roll it out again as thinly as possible and with a pastry wheel or small, sharp knife, trim the dough into a rectangle 16 inches wide by 18 inches long. Cut the rectangle into 2-inch squares.

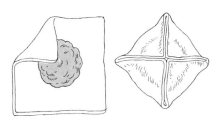

Heap 1 teaspoon of the filling in the center of a square of dough and draw up the four corners to meet in the middle, thus enclosing the filling. Dip your fingers in water and pinch the corners firmly together to seal them. Fill and seal the remaining squares similarly.

Vegetable oil for deep-fat frying

Confectioners' sugar

Fill a deep-fat fryer or deep, heavy pot with enough oil to come 4 inches up the sides of the pan and heat until the oil registers 375° on a deep-fat thermometer. Drop in 10 or 12 fritters, turning them about occasionally with a slotted spoon, fry them for about 3 minutes, or until they are golden brown and crisp. Then drain them on paper towels while you fry the remaining fritters similarly. Arrange the fritters on a serving platter, sprinkle them with confectioners' sugar and serve.

Syrniki *(Russia)*
SWEET CHEESE FRITTERS

To serve 4 to 6

	¼ teaspoon salt
4 cups large-curd pot cheese or	2 tablespoons sugar
cottage cheese (2 pints)	8 tablespoons (¼-pound stick)
4 egg yolks	melted butter
⅔ cup all-purpose flour	1 cup sour cream

Drain the cheese of all its moisture by setting it in a colander, covering it with a kitchen towel, and weighting it with a heavy casserole. Let the cheese drain undisturbed for 2 or 3 hours, then with the back of a spoon, rub it through a fine sieve set over a bowl. Beat in the egg yolks, one at a time, and gradually beat in the flour, salt and sugar. Shape the mixture into 4 equal balls.

One at a time, place the cheese balls on a lightly floured surface and with your hands, form them into 3- or 4-inch-long sausage-shaped cylinders. Wrap each cylinder separately in wax paper and chill for at least 30 minutes.

With a heavy knife, cut each cylinder into 1-inch-wide rounds. Melt 4 tablespoons of the butter in a heavy 10- to 12-inch skillet. Add 6 to 8 rounds to the skillet, and fry over moderate heat for 3 to 5 minutes on each side, or until golden brown. Transfer the *syrniki* to a heated platter and cover them loosely with foil to keep them warm. Fry the remaining rounds similarly, adding butter to the pan as needed. Serve hot, with a bowl of sour cream.

Pannkoogid (*Baltic States*)
DESSERT PANCAKES

To serve 4 (8 to 10 pancakes)

1 cup all-purpose flour	¼ teaspoon salt
2 cups milk	2 egg whites
2 egg yolks	3 tablespoons butter
2 tablespoons sugar	½ cup lingonberry preserves, or
	substitute any berry preserves

Place the flour in a large mixing bowl and, with a large spoon, slowly beat in the milk a half cup at a time. Then beat in the egg yolks, sugar and salt. When the ingredients are thoroughly combined, set the batter aside in a cool —not cold—place for at least 3 hours or even overnight.

Just before making the pancakes, beat the egg whites in a large bowl with a whisk or a rotary or electric beater until they form stiff peaks on the beater when it is lifted out of the bowl. With a rubber spatula, gently but thoroughly fold them into the batter.

Preheat the oven to 250°. With a pastry brush, lightly coat a 5- to 6-inch crêpe pan or skillet with 1 teaspoon of the butter. Pour in ½ cup of the batter, tilting the pan to spread it evenly. Fry over moderate heat for about 3 minutes on each side, until the pancake is golden, turning it over with a spatula. Slide the pancake onto an ovenproof platter and keep it warm in the low oven while you fry the remaining pancakes in similar amounts. Serve the *pannkoogid* on heated dessert plates, accompanied by a bowl of berry preserves.

Paskha (*Russia*)
EASTER CHEESE PYRAMID WITH CANDIED FRUIT AND NUTS

To serve 12 to 16

3 pounds large-curd pot cheese	1 cup heavy cream
½ pound unsalted butter, softened	4 egg yolks
½ cup chopped candied fruits and rinds	1 cup sugar
1 teaspoon vanilla extract	½ cup finely chopped blanched almonds

Drain the pot cheese of all its moisture by setting it in a colander, covering it with cheesecloth or a kitchen towel, and weighting it down with a heavy pot or a small, heavy board. Let the cheese drain for 2 or 3 hours. Meanwhile, combine the candied fruits and the vanilla extract in a small mixing bowl, stir together thoroughly and let the mixture rest for 1 hour. With the back of a wooden spoon, rub the cheese through a fine sieve set over a large bowl. Beat the softened butter thoroughly into the cheese, and set aside.

Over high heat, heat the cream in a small saucepan until small bubbles form around the edge of the pan. Set aside. In a mixing bowl beat the eggs and sugar together with a whisk or a rotary or electric beater until they thicken enough to run sluggishly off the beater when it is lifted out of the bowl. Still beating, slowly add the hot cream in a thin stream, then return the mixture to the pan. Stirring constantly, cook over low heat until the mixture thickens to a custardlike consistency. Do not allow it to boil or it may curdle. Off the heat stir in the candied fruits and set the pan in a large bowl filled with ice cubes covered with 2 inches of water. Stir the custard constantly with a metal spoon until it is completely cooled, then mix it gently but thoroughly into the cheese mixture and stir in the chopped almonds.

Although the Russians use a special *paskha* form in which to shape this Easter dessert a 2-quart clay flower pot with an opening in the bottom is a good substitute. Set the pot in a shallow soup plate and line it with a double thickness of damp cheesecloth, cut long enough so that it hangs at least 2 inches over and around the top of the pot. Pour in the batter and fold the ends of the cheesecloth lightly over the top. Set a weight directly on top of the cheesecloth—perhaps a pan filled with 2 or 3 heavy cans of food—and chill in the refrigerator for at least 8 hours, or overnight, until the dessert is firm.

GARNISH

¼- to ½-cup whole blanched almonds, toasted *(see kulich,*	*page 100)* ¼- to ½-cup candied fruits and rinds

To unmold, unwrap the cheesecloth from the top, invert a flat serving plate on top of the pot and, grasping the two firmly together, turn them over. The *paskha* will slide out easily. Gently peel off the cheesecloth and decorate the top and sides of the cake as fancifully as you like with the almonds and candied fruits.

The *paskha* may be served alone, or spread in a thick layer on slices of *kulich* or on sand cake *(page 95)*. Once unmolded, the *paskha* can be safely kept refrigerated for at least a week before serving.

Khalva *(Caucasus)*
SYRUPY WALNUT DESSERT

To serve 4 to 6

1¾ cups milk
4 tablespoons sugar
1 level tablespoon cornstarch

6 ounces shelled walnuts, cut in half
8 tablespoons (¼-pound stick)
   unsalted butter, melted
½ teaspoon cinnamon

In a 1-quart enameled or stainless-steel saucepan, combine 1½ cups of the milk with the sugar and, stirring constantly, cook over moderate heat until the sugar dissolves. Stir the cornstarch into the remaining milk, then pour into the milk-and-sugar mixture. Bring to a boil and cook until the mixture thickens to a custardlike consistency. Set aside off the heat.

Preheat the oven to 350°. In a mixing bowl, combine the walnuts with the melted butter and toss them with a wooden spoon until they are completely coated. Then spread them out in a shallow, heavy pan just large enough to hold them in one layer. Toast them in the oven for about 20 minutes turning them frequently with a large spoon until they are a deep brown. Watch carefully for any sign of burning. Pour the custard evenly over the nuts, cover the pan securely with foil, and bake in the upper third of the oven 15 or 20 minutes, or until the custard is thick and syrupy. Transfer to small bowls or plates, sprinkle with cinnamon, and serve at once.

Gozinakh *(Caucasus)*
WALNUT HONEY CANDY

To serve 10 to 12

1 pound shelled walnuts, finely
   chopped, or substitute 1 pound

blanched almonds, finely chopped
2 cups (16 ounces) honey
7 tablespoons sugar

Preheat the oven to 350°. Spread the chopped nuts in a single layer in a jelly-roll pan and toast them in the oven for 8 to 10 minutes, turning them about with a spoon from time to time. Watch carefully for any sign of burning.

In a heavy 2-quart pan, combine the honey and sugar and, stirring constantly, bring to a boil. When the syrup reaches 220° on a candy thermometer, lower the heat and stir in the nuts. Stirring often, cook 15 minutes.

Brush the inside of an 8- to 9-inch round pie tin with cold water and pour in the nut mixture. Smooth the top and set aside, uncovered, to cool. When firm, dip the pan into hot water and invert a flat plate on top. Grasping the two firmly together, turn over; the candy should slide out in one piece. With a sharp knife dipped in hot water, cut into diamond shapes. *Gozinakh* will keep at room temperature for 1 week.

Chuchkella (*Caucasus*)
GRAPE-AND-WALNUT CANDIES

To make 2 strings of candy

36 whole walnuts or filberts, shelled	1 tablespoon potato starch dissolved
3 pounds green or purple grapes	in 1 tablespoon cold water

String the walnuts in the following fashion: Tie a knot 1 inch from the ends of two strings each 12 inches long. Then thread the end of one string through the eye of a strong needle. As if you were stringing beads, insert the needle through the center of 18 walnuts. Tie a knot after the last walnut and join the unstrung end of the string into a loop. Thread the second string and loop the other walnuts similarly.

A cup at a time, purée the grapes in an electric blender for about 10 seconds at high speed, or until they liquefy. Strain the purée through a cheese-cloth-lined sieve set over a 2-quart saucepan and discard the grape skins.

To make the purée by hand, rub the grapes through a fine sieve set over the saucepan, pressing down hard on the skins with the back of a spoon before discarding them.

Bring the purée to a boil over high heat, stirring occasionally. Boil briskly, uncovered, for about 15 to 20 minutes, or until the purée has cooked down to 2 cups. Stir in the potato starch-and-water mixture and stirring constantly, cook another minute or two, until the sauce thickens enough to coat a spoon heavily. Set aside.

Holding the looped end, dip the strings of walnuts into the sauce, coating them thoroughly. Hang the loops outdoors where they will dry quickly, or on a towel rack or other spot where they can hang undisturbed; set a plate or napkin beneath to catch the juice drippings. If you are drying them indoors, placing them in front of a fan will speed up the process. When the nuts have dried and are no longer sticky to the touch, warm the juice to lukewarm and dip in the walnuts again. Dry as before, then repeat the dipping and drying process two or three more times, until the nuts are completely coated and there is no longer any separation between them.

Chuchkella are often left hanging for as long as 3 years in the Caucasus. When ready to serve, the sausage-shaped candies are cut crosswise into 1-inch rounds.

Gurev Kasha *(Russia)*
SWEET PUDDING WITH NUTS AND CANDIED FRUITS

To serve 8 to 10

1 quart milk
½ cup sugar
¾ cup semolina or farina
½ teaspoon almond extract
¾ cup walnuts or pecans, pulverized
  with a mortar and pestle or in a
  nut grinder
¾ cup blanched untoasted almonds,
  pulverized with a mortar and pestle
  or in a nut grinder

1 cup apricot preserves
2 tablespoons cold water
1 cup finely chopped mixed candied
  fruits
1 tablespoon unsalted butter,
  softened
30 vanilla wafers, finely crumbled in
  a blender or wrapped in a towel
  and crushed with a rolling pin
  (½ cup)

Combine the milk and sugar in a 1½- to 2-quart saucepan and bring to a boil over moderate heat. Stirring constantly, slowly pour in the semolina or farina, lower the heat and simmer uncovered for about 5 minutes, or until the mixture thickens heavily. Stir in the almond extract and the nuts.

Combine the apricot preserves and 2 tablespoons of cold water in a 1-quart saucepan. Stirring constantly, cook over moderate heat for 1 or 2 minutes, then rub through a fine sieve set over a bowl. Stir in the candied fruits.

Preheat the oven to 350°. With a pastry brush, coat an 8-inch springform pan with the 1 tablespoon of butter. Spoon ⅓ of the semolina mixture into the pan and smooth it out with a spatula. Spread with half the fruit and jam, then make another layer, using half the remaining semolina. Spread the remaining fruit and jam on top and cover with the remaining semolina. Shake the crumbled vanilla wafers through a medium sieve evenly over the top of the pudding.

GARNISH
12 to 16 whole shelled walnuts or
  pecans

10 to 12 glazed whole cherries or
  thin firm slices of stewed fruit,
  such as apples, peaches or pears

Bake in the center of the oven for 30 minutes, or until the top is golden brown. Cool to room temperature. Decorate the top of the pudding in patterns as fancifully as you like with the glazed or stewed fruit and nuts. Remove the springform and refrigerate until ready to serve.

CAKES COOKIES

Liiva Kook *(Baltic States)*
SAND CAKE

To serve 8 to 10

2 teaspoons plus ½ pound unsalted butter, softened
1 tablespoon plus 1 cup all-purpose flour
½ cup sugar
3 eggs
1 cup potato starch
2 teaspoons double-acting baking powder
2 teaspoons brandy
¼ teaspoon vanilla extract
1 ounce blanched sliced almonds, finely chopped

Preheat the oven to 200°. With a pastry brush, coat the bottom and sides of a loaf pan with the 2 teaspoons of butter and sprinkle the pan evenly with 1 tablespoon of flour. Tip the pan from side to side to spread the tablespoon of flour evenly over the buttered surface, then invert the pan and rap it sharply to remove the excess flour.

Cream the ½ pound of butter and sugar together by mashing and beating them against the sides of a bowl with a wooden spoon until light and fluffy. Then beat in the eggs, one at a time, and when they are all absorbed, beat in the potato starch and the cup of flour, ¼ cup at a time. Add the baking powder, brandy and vanilla extract and continue to beat for about 5 minutes, or until the batter is smooth. Stir in the almonds.

Pour the batter into the floured pan, smooth the top with a rubber spatula and bake in the center of the oven for 1 hour, or until the top of the cake is brown and springy to the touch. Run a knife around the inside edge of the pan. Turn the cake out on a wire cake rack. Set another rack on top of the cake and, grasping them firmly together, invert them. Let the cake cool to room temperature, transfer it to a cake plate and serve as a breakfast "bread" with unsalted butter, or as a dessert with whipped cream.

Romovaia Baba *(Russia)*

BABA AU RHUM: RUM-SOAKED CAKE WITH CURRANTS AND RAISINS

To serve 10 to 12

2 packages active dry yeast	8 eggs, lightly beaten
⅓ cup sugar	¾ pound plus 2 tablespoons
1 cup lukewarm milk (110° to 115°)	unsalted butter, softened
1 teaspoon salt	½ cup dried currants (2 ounces)
4 cups sifted all-purpose flour	¼ cup sultana raisins (1 ounce)

In a small, shallow bowl, sprinkle the yeast and ½ teaspoon of the sugar over ½ cup of the lukewarm milk. Let the mixture stand for 2 or 3 minutes, then stir to dissolve the yeast completely. Set the bowl aside in a warm, draft-free place, such as an unlighted oven, for 5 to 8 minutes, or until the mixture has doubled in volume.

In a deep mixing bowl, combine the remaining sugar with the salt and flour. Make a well in the center and pour in the yeast mixture. Add the remaining milk, drop in the eggs and with a large spoon stir the flour into the liquid ingredients. Continue to stir until a fairly soft, sticky dough is formed. Then beat the dough with your hands for about 10 minutes by slapping it against the bowl, pulling it up high out of the bowl and letting it fall back on itself as you proceed. Drape the bowl with a kitchen towel and set it in the warm, draft-free place for 1 hour, or until the dough doubles in bulk. Punch it down and knead in ¾ pound of the softened butter, a tablespoon or so at a time. Knead in the currants and raisins.

With a pastry brush, coat the inside of a 12-cup *kugelhof* mold with the remaining 2 tablespoons of softened butter. Pat the dough into the mold; it should come about halfway up the sides. Cover the mold loosely with a kitchen towel and set aside in the warm, draft-free place for about 1 hour, or until the dough has doubled in volume and has risen almost to the top of the pan. Preheat the oven to 400°.

Bake the cake in the center of the oven for 10 minutes, then lower the heat to 350° and bake another 35 minutes. Remove from the oven, drape a kitchen towel loosely over the top of the mold and let it rest for 5 minutes. Run a knife around the inside edge of the mold and turn the cake out into a deep serving dish. Then carefully turn the cake over on the plate.

SYRUP	1½ cups water
2 cups sugar	1 cup dark rum

SYRUP: Combine the sugar and water in a small saucepan and, stirring constantly, bring to a boil over high heat. Cook briskly for 5 minutes, undisturbed, until the mixture forms a syrup thick enough to coat a spoon lightly. Pour the syrup into a bowl, then stir in the rum.

ICING (optional)   1 recipe white icing *(see kulich, page 100)*

Slowly spoon the warm syrup over the warm cake. With a large spoon, baste the cake every 10 minutes or so with the syrup collecting around the cake. When all the syrup has been absorbed, you may, if you like, ice the top of the cake with the white icing just before serving.

Béržo Šakà *(Baltic States)*
BIRCH LOG

To serve 8 to 10

CAKE	
2 tablespoons unsalted butter, softened	2 tablespoons fresh strained lemon juice
5 egg whites	Grated rind of 1 lemon (about 1 tablespoon)
5 egg yolks	½ cup all-purpose flour
¾ cup sugar	½ teaspoon baking powder

CAKE: Brush a tablespoon of softened butter over the bottom and sides of a jelly-roll pan. Line the pan with a 22-inch strip of wax paper letting the extra paper extend over each edge of the pan. Brush the remaining tablespoon of butter over the paper in the pan (but not on the overhanging strips) and scatter a small handful of flour over it. Tip the pan from side to side to spread the flour evenly. Then turn the pan over and rap it to dislodge the excess flour.

Preheat the oven to 350°. In a mixing bowl, beat the egg whites with a whisk or a rotary or electric beater until they form firm, unwavering peaks when the beater is lifted from the bowl. In another small bowl, beat the egg yolks briefly with the unwashed beater and beat in the sugar, lemon juice and lemon rind until well combined. Mix a large tablespoon of the whites into the yolks, then pour the mixture over the remaining whites and fold together gently. Alternately fold in the flour and baking powder until the ingredients are well combined. Do not overfold.

Pour the batter into the jelly-roll pan and spread it evenly into the corners with a rubber spatula. Bake in the middle of the oven for about 20 minutes, or until the cake draws slightly away from the sides of the pan and a small knife inserted in its center comes out dry and clean. Turn the cake out on a sheet of wax paper, then gently peel off the top layer of paper. Let the cake cool to room temperature before filling and rolling it.

Continued on next page

FILLING

12 ounces pitted prunes
12 tablespoons (1½ quarter-pound
    sticks) unsalted butter, softened
⅔ cup sugar

1 egg yolk
½ teaspoon vanilla extract
2 ounces semisweet chocolate,
    melted and cooled

FILLING: While the cake is cooling, prepare the filling. In a 1½- to 2-quart saucepan combine the prunes with enough cold water to cover them completely. Bring to a boil over high heat. Then lower the heat and simmer uncovered about 15 minutes, or until the prunes are soft. Drain the prunes and purée them through a food mill, or rub them with the back of a spoon through a fine sieve set over a bowl. Discard the skins.

Cream the butter and sugar together by beating them against the sides of a mixing bowl with a wooden spoon. Beat in the egg yolk, prune purée, vanilla extract and the cooled melted chocolate. Continue to beat until the filling is smooth.

With a rubber spatula, spread the filling evenly to all edges of the cake. Cut off a 2-inch strip from one end of the cake and put it aside. Using the wax paper to help you, roll the cake jelly-roll fashion into a long cylinder. Spread and roll the smaller section similarly and refrigerate them both, lightly wrapped in wax paper, for about 30 minutes, or until the fillings are firm.

FROSTING

3 egg whites
Pinch of cream of tartar
2 cups confectioners' sugar, sifted

1 teaspoon fresh strained lemon juice
1 ounce semisweet chocolate, melted
    and cooled

FROSTING: In a large mixing bowl, beat the egg whites and the cream of tartar until the whites form soft peaks on the beater. Still beating, slowly pour in the sugar and the lemon juice and continue to beat until the whites are stiff and glossy. With a spatula, spread the frosting evenly over the surface of both the large and small rolls.

Cut the small roll into 1½- to 2-inch-long sections and attach the cut ends to the "log" at angles every 2 or 3 inches along its length, imitating stubs of branches. Dip the prongs of a fork into the melted chocolate and run the prongs down the length of the log and around the stubs, thus making birch bark markings. Refrigerate the birch log until ready to serve.

Medivnyk *(Ukraine)*

SPICED HONEY CAKE

To serve 6 to 8

¾ cup honey
½ teaspoon powdered cinnamon
¼ teaspoon powdered cloves
¼ teaspoon powdered nutmeg
1 teaspoon baking soda
4 tablespoons unsalted butter, softened
½ cup dark brown sugar

3 egg yolks
2 cups flour
¼ teaspoon salt
1 teaspoon baking powder
10 tablespoons raisins
6 tablespoons dried currants
½ cup finely chopped walnuts
3 egg whites
3 tablespoons butter, softened

NOTE: *Medivnyk* should be made 1 or 2 days before you plan to serve it, to allow the flavor to develop properly.

In a 1- to 1½-quart saucepan bring the honey to a boil over moderate heat, stirring almost constantly with a wooden spoon. Stir in the cinnamon, cloves, nutmeg and baking soda and set aside to cool to room temperature.

In a large bowl, cream the 4 tablespoons of butter and the sugar together by mashing and beating them against the sides of the bowl with a large spoon until they are light and fluffy. Then beat in the egg yolks, one at a time, and stir in the cooled, spiced honey. Combine 1¾ cups of the flour with the salt and baking powder and beat them into the sugar-and-egg mixture, ¼ cup at a time. Combine the raisins, currants and walnuts in a separate mixing bowl and toss them with the remaining ¼ cup of flour until each piece is coated. Fold into the batter.

Preheat the oven to 300°. Beat the egg whites in a large bowl with a whisk or a rotary or electric beater, until they form stiff peaks on the beater when lifted out of the bowl. With a rubber spatula, gently fold the egg whites into the batter, using an over-and-under folding motion rather than a mixing motion. With a pastry brush and 2 tablespoons of the softened butter, coat the bottom and sides of a 9-by-5-by-3-inch loaf pan. Coat both sides of a sheet of brown paper with the remaining tablespoon of butter and line the sides of the pan with it. Pour the batter into the pan and bake in the center of the oven for 1½ hours, or until a toothpick or cake tester inserted into the center of the cake comes out clean. With a knife, loosen the sides of the cake from the pan and invert the cake onto a cake rack. Let the cake cool to room temperature, then cover loosely with wax paper and set aside for 1 or 2 days at room temperature before slicing.

Kulich *(Russia)*

EASTER COFFEE CAKE WITH NUTS AND RAISINS

To serve 10 to 12

1 cup lukewarm milk (110° to 115°)	10 egg yolks
3 packages active dry yeast	½ teaspoon powdered saffron
½ teaspoon sugar	½ pound unsalted butter, cut into
½ cup sultana raisins	small bits and softened
¼ cup rum	½ cup slivered or coarsely chopped
2 cups confectioners' sugar	blanched almonds
3½ to 5 cups all-purpose flour	½ cup mixed candied fruits and
1 teaspoon vanilla extract	rinds
	3 tablespoons butter, softened

Pour ½ cup of the lukewarm milk into a small, shallow bowl and sprinkle it with the yeast and the ½ teaspoon sugar. Let the mixture stand for 2 or 3 minutes, then stir to dissolve the yeast completely. Set the bowl aside in a warm, draft-free place (such as an unlighted oven) for about 10 minutes, or until the mixture almost doubles in volume.

Soak the sultana raisins in the rum for at least 10 minutes.

Preheat the oven to 400°. Sift the confectioners' sugar and 3½ cups of the flour through a fine sieve set over a large mixing bowl. Slowly pour in the dissolved yeast mixture and the remaining ½ cup of milk, stirring constantly until a stiff batter is formed. Beat in the vanilla and the egg yolks, one at a time. When the mixture becomes too stiff to stir, knead it vigorously with your hands until the dough is smooth and elastic.

With a slotted spoon, remove the raisins from the rum and spread them out on paper towels to drain. Then dissolve the saffron in the rum and pour the saffron and rum over the dough. Knead the dough with your hands until all the liquid is absorbed, and knead or beat in the butter, a few bits at a time, until well combined.

Gather the dough into a compact ball and place it on a lightly floured surface. Knead it by pushing it down with the heels of your hands, pressing it forward, and folding it back on itself. Repeat this process for about 10 minutes. If the dough begins to stick at any point, add as much of the additional flour as you need, ½ cup at a time. Continue to knead until the dough is satiny and elastic, then gather it into a ball again. Place it in a lightly buttered bowl, dust the top lightly with flour and cover the bowl with a kitchen towel. Set aside in the warm, draft-free place for about 1 hour, or until the dough doubles in volume.

Meanwhile, spread the almonds out in a single layer in a cake tin and toast them in the oven for 5 minutes, or until they are lightly and evenly colored, turning them from time to time. In a small bowl, combine the almonds with the candied fruits and raisins. Sprinkle them with a tablespoon of flour and toss them together with your hands.

With a sharp blow of your fist, punch the dough down in the bowl. Add the fruit mixture and knead vigorously until the mixture is more or less evenly distributed throughout the dough.

With a can opener, remove and discard the bottom of an empty can about 6 inches wide and 7 inches high—such as a 3-pound coffee tin. With a pastry brush, coat the bottom and sides of the tin with 2 tablespoons of the softened butter. Spread 1 tablespoon of butter on a sheet of heavy brown paper about 22 inches long and use it, unbuttered side in, to line the tin. Let the excess paper hang over the top of the tin, and tie it around with kitchen cord.

Set the tin on a cookie sheet or baking tin and drop in the ball of dough. Cover it loosely with a kitchen towel and set the mold aside in the warm, draft-free spot for another 30 minutes, or until it again doubles in volume and has risen almost to the top of the mold. Bake in the center of the 400° oven for 15 minutes, then lower the temperature to 350° and bake one hour. The cake will mushroom over the top of the tin and form a cap. Remove the tin from the oven and carefully lift out the cake. Set it upright on a wire cake rack to cool.

WHITE ICING

2 cups confectioners' sugar   2 teaspoons fresh, strained lemon
¼ cup cold water   juice

ICING: With a wooden spoon, mix together the sugar, water and lemon juice and pour it over the top of the warm cake, allowing it to run down the cake in thin streams.

The Russians prepare *kulich* for serving by first slicing off the mushroom-shaped cap and placing it in the center of a large serving platter. The cake is cut in half lengthwise and finally cut crosswise into 1½- to 2-inch-thick slices. The slices are then arranged around the top of the cake. A traditional accompaniment is *paskha (page 90)*.

Smetanik *(Russia)*

BERRY JAM AND SOUR-CREAM PIE

To serve 8

PASTRY DOUGH

8 tablespoons (¼-pound stick) unsalted butter, cut into ¼-inch bits and chilled	shortening
	2¼ cups all-purpose flour
	¼ teaspoon salt
3 tablespoons chilled vegetable	5 to 7 tablespoons ice water

PASTRY: In a large mixing bowl, combine the butter, vegetable shortening, flour and salt. Working quickly, use your fingertips to rub the flour and fat together until they blend and look like flakes of coarse meal. Pour 5 tablespoons of ice water over the mixture all at once, toss together lightly and gather the dough into a ball. If the dough crumbles, add up to 2 more tablespoons of ice water by drops until the particles adhere. Divide the dough in half, dust each half lightly with flour and wrap separately in sheets of wax paper. Refrigerate for at least 3 hours, or until firm.

FILLING

2 cups finely ground almonds, lightly toasted	2 egg yolks
	⅓ cup sour cream
4 teaspoons milk	2 teaspoons cinnamon
6 tablespoons raspberry jam	1 tablespoon unsalted butter,
6 tablespoons cherry jam	softened

FILLING: Soak the almonds in the milk for 5 to 10 minutes. With the back of a large spoon, rub the raspberry and cherry jams through a fine sieve set over a large bowl. Then beat in it the egg yolks, sour cream, cinnamon, the nuts and their soaking milk.

On a lightly floured surface, roll the dough into a 12-inch circle about ⅛ inch thick. With a pastry brush, coat the bottom and sides of a 9-inch false-bottomed tart pan with the tablespoon of softened butter. Drape the pastry over the rolling pin, lift it up and unfold it slackly over the pan. Gently press the pastry into the bottom and around the sides of the pan, being careful not to stretch it. Roll the pin over the rim of the pan, pressing down hard to trim off the excess pastry.

Preheat the oven to 425°. Pour the filling into the pastry shell and roll out the other half of dough into a 12-inch circle. Drape it over the rolling pin, lift it up and unfold it over the filling. Press the edges of the pastry layers together. Then crimp them with your fingers or press them firmly around the rim with the prongs of a fork. With a sharp knife, cut three 1-inch slits about 1 inch apart in the top of the pastry. Bake in the center of the oven for 30 minutes, or until the pastry is golden brown. Then set the pan on a large jar or coffee can and carefully slip off the outside rim. Let the pie cool to room temperature before serving.

Mazurka (*Russia*)
EASTER NUT CAKE

To serve 8 to 10

1 tablespoon unsalted butter, softened	1 tablespoon fresh strained lemon juice
5 egg yolks	1/2 pound toasted hazel nuts, shelled and pulverized in a mortar and pestle or in a nut grinder
3/4 cup superfine sugar	
Grated rind of 1 lemon (about 1 tablespoon)	5 egg whites

Preheat the oven to 375°. With a pastry brush, butter the bottom and sides of an 8-inch-wide, 3-inch-deep springform cake pan with the tablespoon of softened butter. With a whisk or a rotary or electric beater, beat the egg yolks for about 1 minute, then slowly pour in the sugar. Continue beating until the mixture falls back upon itself in a ribbon when the beater is lifted out of the bowl. Beat in the grated lemon rind and lemon juice, and with a rubber spatula, fold in the hazel nuts.

In another bowl, and with a clean beater, beat the egg whites until they form firm, unwavering peaks on the beater when it is lifted out of the bowl. Gently but thoroughly fold the whites into the egg-yolk mixture until no streaks of white show. Pour the batter into the buttered pan and spread evenly to the sides with the spatula. Bake in the center of the oven for about 40 minutes, or until it has puffed and has begun to come slightly away from the sides of the pan. Turn off the heat and let the cake rest in the oven for 15 minutes. Remove the sides of the pan and turn the cake out on a cake rack. Cool to room temperature.

TOPPING	2 tablespoons rum
1 cup heavy cream, chilled	2 tablespoons confectioners' sugar

To make the topping, beat the cream with a whisk or a rotary or electric beater until it forms soft peaks. Then gradually beat in the rum and sugar and continue to beat until stiff. With a spatula, spread it over the top of the cake and serve at once.

Aleksander Torte *(Baltic States)*

RASPBERRY-FILLED PASTRY STRIPS

To make about 4 dozen

½ pound unsalted butter, chilled and cut into bits	1 egg
3 to 3½ cups all-purpose flour	1½ cups (12 ounces) raspberry preserves
3 tablespoons sugar	2 tablespoons softened butter

In a large mixing bowl, combine the chilled butter, 3 cups of the flour and the sugar and, with your fingertips, rub until the mixture resembles flakes of coarse meal. Beat in the egg and continue to mix until the pastry is smooth. Shape it into a ball, wrap it in wax paper, and refrigerate 1 hour, or until the dough is firm.

With the back of a spoon, rub the preserves through a fine sieve set over a 1-quart saucepan, then cook over moderate heat, stirring constantly, for 3 to 5 minutes, or until they thicken into a thin purée. Set aside off the heat.

Preheat the oven to 250°. Cut the chilled pastry in half and shape each half into a rectangle. One half at a time, roll the pastry between two sheets of lightly floured wax paper into a rectangle approximately 10 inches wide and 15 inches long. With a pastry brush, coat each of 2 cookie sheets with 1 tablespoon of butter and sprinkle them with flour, tipping the sheets from side to side to coat them evenly. Then invert the sheets and tap them against a hard surface to dislodge any excess flour. Following the pictures opposite, use the wax paper to lift the pastry onto the sheets. Bake 40 minutes, or until the pastry begins to turn a pale gold. Watch carefully for any sign of burning and regulate the heat accordingly.

With a metal spatula, spread the raspberry purée evenly over one sheet of the pastry, covering it completely and smoothly. Slide the second sheet of pastry gently onto the first.

WHITE ICING	¼ cup cold water
2 cups confectioners' sugar	2 teaspoons lemon juice

With a spoon stir the sugar, water and lemon juice together in a large mixing bowl to form a thin paste. Spread the icing smoothly over the top layer of pastry with the spatula, and set the cake aside to cool to room temperature. With a small, sharp knife or pastry wheel, slice the *Aleksander torte* into strips 1 inch wide and 2 inches long.

Roll half of the delicate *Aleksander torte* pastry between two sheets of lightly floured wax paper.

To make a 10-by-15-inch rectangle, fold in any excess edges, cover with wax paper again and roll smooth.

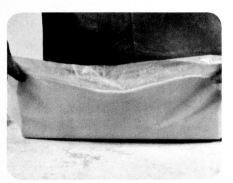

Peel off the top sheet of wax paper and use the bottom one to lift the pastry onto a cookie sheet.

Similarly roll the remaining dough and bake each separately. Spread one layer evenly with raspberry purée.

Gently slide the second layer of pastry off its cookie sheet onto the raspberry-covered layer.

Cover the top layer of pastry with lemon-flavored sugar icing, cool, then slice into 1-by-2-inch strips.

Krendel *(Russia)*

PRETZEL WITH FRUITS AND NUTS

To serve 10 to 12

1 recipe for *kulich* dough *(page 100)*
1 tablespoon softened butter
½ cup blanched almonds, pulverized

in a mortar and pestle or firmly
ground with a nut grinder
Confectioners' sugar

Preheat the oven to 400°. Prepare the yeast dough as described on page 100. After the dough has risen to double its volume and you have punched it down with your fist, place it on a large, lightly floured surface—the largest you have. With lightly floured hands shape the dough into a long rope, making the center twice as thick as the ends. The tips of the rope should be about ½ inch thick, and the rope should be at least 60 inches long. To use less working surface, form the rope into a semicircle as you shape it.

With a pastry brush, coat a large cookie sheet with 1 tablespoon of butter. Carefully transfer the rope of dough to the long side of the cookie sheet. Following the drawings below, draw the ends of the rope down, then cross them over each other and twist the ends 3 or 4 times. Tuck the tips of this braid under the thick middle of the rope.

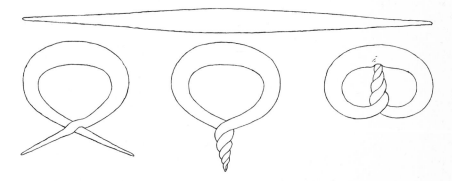

Place the dough in a warm, draft-free place (such as an unlighted oven) for 20 minutes, or until it has risen and almost doubled in volume. Sprinkle the top evenly with the ground almonds and bake in the center of the oven for 15 minutes. Lower the heat to 350°, and bake an additional 45 minutes, or until the top of the pretzel is a deep rich brown. Sprinkle with confectioners' sugar and slide the pretzel onto a wire cake rack to cool. *Krendel* is traditionally served in many parts of the Soviet Union on saints' days and similar family celebrations.

Shokoladno-Mindalnyi Tort s Kofeinym Kremom *(Russia)*

CHOCOLATE ALMOND TORTE WITH MOCHA FROSTING

To serve 8 to 10

CAKE

1 tablespoon butter, softened
¼ cup all-purpose flour
½ pound unsalted butter, softened
2 cups sugar
4 egg yolks
½ cup heavy cream
1 cup mashed or riced boiled
   potatoes, cooled to room
   temperature
1 cup almonds, pulverized in a

mortar and pestle or in a nut
   grinder
4 ounces unsweetened chocolate,
   melted and cooled to lukewarm
1 teaspoon powdered cinnamon
2 tablespoons rum
1½ cups cake flour (not self-rising)
2 teaspoons baking powder
1 teaspoon vanilla extract
4 egg whites

Preheat the oven to 325°. With a pastry brush, lightly coat the bottom and sides of an 8-inch wide, 3-inch deep springform cake pan with the tablespoon of butter. Add the ¼ cup of all-purpose flour and tip the pan from side to side to coat it evenly. Invert the pan and rap it sharply to dislodge any excess flour.

In a large mixing bowl, cream the ½ pound of butter and the sugar together by beating them against the sides of the bowl with a wooden spoon until smooth and fluffy. Beat in the egg yolks, one at a time, then beat in the heavy cream, potatoes, almonds, melted chocolate, cinnamon, rum, cake flour, baking powder and vanilla extract.

In another large bowl, beat the egg whites with a whisk or a rotary or electric beater until they form firm, unwavering peaks when the beater is lifted from the bowl. With a rubber spatula, gently but thoroughly fold the egg whites into the batter. Then pour it into the springform pan and smooth it with a spatula.

Bake in the center of the oven for 1 to 1½ hours, or until the cake has puffed and a cake tester inserted in its center comes out clean. Remove the sides of the pan and let the torte cool to room temperature. Then with a serrated knife slice it into 2 layers.

FILLING

½ cup apricot preserves

While the cake is baking, prepare the filling and frosting. Dissolve the apricot preserves in a small pan set over moderate heat. With the back of a large spoon, rub them through a fine sieve set over a small bowl. Set aside.

Continued on next page

MOCHA FROSTING

3 tablespoons unsalted butter, softened

1½ cups confectioners' sugar

2 tablespoons leftover strong coffee, or use 1 teaspoon instant coffee dissolved in 2 tablespoons boiling water, then cooled

1 ounce unsweetened chocolate, melted and cooled

1 tablespoon dark rum

½ teaspoon vanilla extract

In a small mixing bowl, cream the butter and sugar together by beating them vigorously against the sides of the bowl with a wooden spoon. Beat in the coffee, melted chocolate, rum and vanilla extract. Cover with plastic wrap and chill for 15 to 20 minutes, or until the frosting is firm enough to spread easily.

With a spatula, spread the apricots over one layer of the cake. Set the second layer on top and spread the surface of the torte with the mocha frosting.

NOTE: Size, weight and material are specified for pans in the recipes because they affect cooking results. A pan should be just large enough to hold its contents comfortably. Heavy pans heat slowly and cook food at a constant rate. Aluminum and cast iron conduct heat well but may discolor foods containing egg yolks, wine, vinegar or lemon. Enamelware is a fairly poor conductor of heat. Many recipes therefore recommend stainless steel or enameled cast iron, which do not have these faults.

Recipe Index: English

Recipe Index: Foreign

First Courses

Soups

Salads and Vegetables

Fish

Poultry

Meats

Rice and Kasha

Breads and Dumplings

Candies and Desserts

Cakes and Cookies

Drawings by Matt Greene, photographs by Fred Eng.   Printed in U.S.A.